Frank H. Tompkins

The Mississippi River

The commercial highway of the nation. The improvement of its navigation and the control of its flood waters.

Frank H. Tompkins

The Mississippi River
The commercial highway of the nation. The improvement of its navigation and the control of its flood waters.

ISBN/EAN: 9783337105860

Printed in Europe, USA, Canada, Australia, Japan

Cover: Foto ©ninafisch / pixelio.de

More available books at **www.hansebooks.com**

THE MISSISSIPPI RIVER.

THE COMMERCIAL HIGHWAY OF THE NATION.

THE IMPROVEMENT OF ITS NAVIGATION AND THE CONTROL OF ITS FLOOD WATERS.

EDITED BY
FRANK H. TOMPKINS,
OF LOUISIANA.

Republished from the *Manufacturers' Record*,
BALTIMORE, MD.
1892.

PREFACE.

The articles published in this work—most of them written by able engineers and public men, and treating of some of the phases of "The Mississippi River Question"—are reproduced from the columns of the *Manufacturers' Record*. Only such articles are incorporated in this volume as bear on the science of levees; their necessity as adjuncts to navigation, and the successful treatment of the Mississippi river; and the constitutional questions involved. No attempt is made to include the thorough exposition of the possibilities of development—commercial, mechanical and agricultural—of this vast empire of 26,000,000 acres of alluvium. This is one of the greatest questions that to-day confront the American people; and its solution means millions added to the producing capacity of our country, and millions annually saved to the agriculturists of the twenty-five States drained by the great Mississippi and its tributaries.

INTRODUCTORY ARTICLE ON MISSISSIPPI RIVER IMPROVEMENT.

[Written for the *Manufacturers' Record* by Hon. T. C. Catchings, M. C.]

The exploits of Cortes in Mexico and Pizarro in Peru excited the attention of the European States to a degree which surpasses description. Spain and Portugal especially were fired with an enthusiasm for further conquest which knew no bounds. Those eager for adventure and military renown, and those whose imaginations were inflamed by the belief that exhaustless treasure awaited discovery, were alike active in organizing expeditions to explore the newly-found America.

One of these, led by Ponce de Leon, who had been a companion of Columbus, set out from Porto Rico in March, 1512, in search of the Fountain of Youth, whose waters were supposed to baffle time and disease, and make youth perpetual.

It landed near St. Augustine, where it was set upon by the natives with intense fury. Those who were not slain were driven to their ships and returned to Cuba, where Ponce de Leon, who had been mortally wounded, soon died.

Bancroft says : "So ended the adventurer who had coveted immeasurable wealth and hoped for perpetual youth. The discoverer of Florida had desired immortality on earth and gained only its shadow." Other expeditions followed, which met with no better fortune.

In the year 1538 Hernando De Soto, one of the conquerors of Peru, surpassed in military renown only by Pizarro and Cortes, a Spanish nobleman of great wealth and influence, procured from the Emperor of Spain authority to undertake the conquest of Florida at his own expense. Attracted by the splendid promise of glory and riches, which such a movement commanded by so renowned and brilliant a captain offered, De Soto had no difficulty in gathering about him a band of bold, ambitious and courageous men, filled with enthusiasm and eager to follow wheresoever he might lead.

Mr. Irving says of this enterprise: "It was poetry put into action; it was the knight-errantry of the Old World carried into the depths of the American wilderness. The personal adventures, the feats of individual prowess, the picturesque descriptions of steel-clad cavaliers with lance and helm and prancing steed glittering through the wildernesses of Florida, Georgia, Alabama and the prairies of the far West would seem to us mere fictions of romance did they not come to us in the matter-of-fact narratives of those who were eye-witnesses and who recorded minute memoranda of every day's incidents." The expedition set sail from Havana, May 12, 1539, and arrived in the bay of Espiritu Santo on the 25th of the same month.

It is needless to recount the many adventures of the expedition, but from the moment of its landing on the coast of Florida until its return four years later, its history is a story of continuous privation, suffering and sanguinary conflict. Engaged almost daily in combat with the natives, confronted constantly by dangers and difficulties of every conceivable nature, this gallant band of cavaliers forced their way, step by step, through the wilds of Florida, Georgia, Alabama and Mississippi, until they reached the banks of the Mississippi river in April, 1541, at a point near the present city of Helena. Because of its size they called it the "Rio Grande."

They crossed the river and pushed on westward, but were compelled by many disasters to return, and reached it again in May, 1542. Here on June 5, in his 42d year, Hernando De Soto, the first European who beheld the mighty and noble stream, worn out by incessant fatigue of body and mind, ended his career, and his companions, placing his body in a coffin made by hollowing out a piece of green oak, took it out to the middle of the river and sunk it in nineteen fathoms of water. Thinking to reach Mexico, his survivors again marched westward, but were driven back by stress of circumstances, and returned to the river at a point near the mouth of the Arkansas.

Reduced in numbers to less than 350 men, they determined to abandon all further efforts of exploration, and constructed a small fleet of boats, in which they embarked on July 2, 1543. After passing through many dangers they reached the sea twenty days later, and beat their way westward until they reached the town of Panuco, on the Mexican coast, where they disbanded.

It was through this expedition that we get our first knowledge of the Mississippi river, and its description given then will answer for to-day.

Monette says: "The lapse of three centuries has not changed the character of the stream. It was then described as it now is, as more than a mile in width, flowing with a strong current, and by the weight of its waters forcing a channel of great depth. The water was described as being always muddy, and trees and timber were continually floating down the stream."

While Spain was attempting the conquest of the Southern country, and England that along the New England and Middle Atlantic coast, France had gained a foothold in the extreme North, and had founded the city of Quebec as early as 1608.

The motive which impelled her was very different, however, from that which controlled other powers.

Bancroft truly says: "It was neither commercial enterprise nor royal ambition which carried the power of France into the heart of our continent. The motive was religion." We therefore naturally find that the Jesuits were always on the outposts of French progress. "The history of their labors is connected with the origin of every celebrated town in the annals of French America. Not a river was entered, not a cape was turned, but a Jesuit led the way."

In 1669 Father Allouez learned from the tribes of Indians on the southern shores of Lake Superior of a great river further to the west called by them the "Mesasippi" or Great River.

It was ascertained "that it flowed neither toward the north nor toward the east," but not to what point its course lay, nor into what sea it discharged.

In 1673 an expedition to discover and explore this great river was organized. It was put in charge of M. Joliet, of Quebec, and Father Marquette, who had aided in establishing a mission at the Sault St. Marie.

The latter, by reason of his familiarity with the natives and their great attachment to him, was well fitted to lead such an enterprise. "Such was the veneration of the savages for this good man, that for years after his death, when overtaken in their frail bark canoes by the storms on Lake Michigan, it is said that they called upon the name of Marquette, and the winds ceased and the waves were still."

They turned from Lake Michigan into Green Bay, where they entered and ascended Fox river. Thence they crossed the portage to the Wisconsin, and descending it, reached the Mississippi June 17, 1673.

They passed the mouth of the Missouri, (the Pekitanoni of the Indians,) the confluence of the Ohio, and down the river 1,100 miles below the point at which they had entered it. They then returned and made known their discovery amidst great rejoicing. Until then no white man had seen the Mississippi since the fatal expedition of De Soto, one hundred and thirty years before.

La Salle, in 1679, next entered the river, but he crossed the portage from Lake Michigan into the Illinois, and went down that stream. He caused explorations to be made as far up as St. Anthony's Falls, and in 1682 descended to the Gulf of Mexico.

He named the river "St. Louis," and the country, "Louisiana." Returning to France, he organized a colony and sailed for the mouth of the river, but failed to find it, and landed at the Bay of Matagorda. While attempting to reach the settlement which he had founded on the Illinois before returning to France, he was slain by his companions. In 1689 De Tonti descended to the mouth of the river in search of La Salle, but hearing nothing of him regained the Illinois country. Owing to continuous Indian wars, no further discoveries were made until about the treaty of 1700, with the five nations, which is described as follows: "A written treaty was made, to which each nation placed for itself a symbol— the Senecas and Onondagas drew a spider; the Cayugas a calumet; the Oneidas a forked stick, and the Mohawks a bear." After this colonies began to enter the valley both from the North and the South.

Towns and trading posts were established, especially in the Illinois country, and as early as 1712 land titles and deeds came into use to designate private acquisitions. By 1720 a very considerable trade had grown up between the upper and the lower settlements.

Iberville established a post at Biloxi in 1699, and made repeated explorations of the lakes, bayous and tributaries of the lower river.

The movements of the French had attracted the attention of the English to the Mississippi valley, and they dispatched a man-of-war about this time to explore the mouths of the river. Bienville, a subordinate of Iberville, while sounding the channel a few miles below the site of New Orleans, met this vessel and threatened resistance if it did not leave. The vessel departed, though under protest, and the point at which it turned is known to this day as the "English Turn." New Orleans was founded in 1718, and a survey of the passes by Pauger, a royal French engineer, having shown that shipping could be brought up the river, it was made the principal depot and capital of Louisiana.

The commerce of the valley in 1745 is thus described. "The trade between the northern and southern portions of Louisiana had greatly augmented, as well as that from New Orleans to France and foreign countries. Regular cargoes of flour, bacon, pork, hides, leather, tallow, bear's oil and lumber were annually transported down the Mississippi in keel boats and barges to New Orleans and Mobile, whence they were shipped to France and the West Indies. In their return voyages these boats and barges, from New Orleans and Mobile, supplied the Illinois and Wabash countries with rice, indigo, tobacco, sugar, cotton and European fabrics. The two extremes of Louisiana produced and supplied each other alternately with the necessaries and comforts of life required by each respectively. The mutual exchange of commodities kept up a constant and active communication from one end of the province to the other. Boats, barges and pirogues were daily plying from one point to another, freighted with the rude products of a new and growing country. The great highways of commerce were the deep and solitary channels of the Mississippi and its hundreds of tributaries."

In the lower country rice, indigo and tobacco were the chief crops at this time. In 1751 sugar cane began to be cultivated. The first sugar mill was erected in 1758 and proved so remunerative that many others were put up, and by 1760 sugar cane had become one of the staple crops. Cotton was grown, but only in limited quantities for domestic consumption, because of the difficulty in separating the lint from the seed. About 1752 a cotton gin was invented by M. Dubreuil, which so facilitated the process that cotton growing became more extensive. But it was not until the invention in 1807 by Whitney of the saw cotton gin that the impulse to cotton growing was given, which has made it the chief business of many portions of the South.

Only the large plantations, however, could afford a gin, so public gins were set up, upon which the crops of the small planters were ginned.

In the Mississippi territory, laws were passed requiring all cotton to be ginned within four months from its delivery. "Cotton receipts" were given, and as early as March, 1806, they were made negotiable by law, whereby they became domestic bills of exchange and answered the purpose of a circulating medium.

A continued struggle had been progressing for supremacy in the Mississippi valley between France, England and Spain, with various and shifting results, which need not be recited here.

By the treaty of 1783, Great Britain relinquished to

the United States everything east of the Mississippi, from its source to the 31st parallel of north latitude, and at the same time it ceded to Spain everything east of the Mississippi and south of the 31st parallel. France, in 1763, had ceded to Spain all Western Louisiana, including the island of Orleans.

Thus the river for the last 300 miles flowed entirely through Spanish dominions, and Spain claimed the exclusive right to the use of that portion, and imposed heavy duties on all produce brought down. They were enforced by excise officers, supported by the military, and every boat was required to land and submit to these revenue exactions.

This was the only outlet for the rapidly-growing West, and the American people demanded free navigation as a natural right, as well as through the treaty with Great Britain.

In 1788, Congress declared "that the free navigation of the Mississippi is a clear and essential right of the United States, and that the same ought to be considered and supported as such."

Finally, Spain, by the treaty of 1795, stipulated "that the whole width of said river, from its source to the sea, shall be free to the people of the United States."

France had never approved the cession to Spain of Western Louisiana, and Napoleon, by the treaty of Ildefonso, confirmed in March, 1801, required it from Spain. Being involved in war with England, however, and apprehensive that he could not hold it, by the treaty of 1803, he sold it to the United States. When the treaty had been executed, he said: "This accession of territory strengthens forever the power of the United States, and I have just given to England a maritime rival that will sooner or later humble her pride."

From this time on, and especially after the introduction of steam power, the commerce of the river rapidly increased, and to-day its valley is the center of wealth, population and political control.

Just above Cairo, 1,100 miles from the mouth, the river cuts through a spur of the Ozark mountains. The whole area of the valley up to this point was at one time covered by sea water, which has been gradually displaced by the sediment brought from above by the river. It is still subject to overflow by the floods, which at time pour down to the sea.

The river, indeed, is the great outlet to carry off the surplus waters of the vast region between the Rocky and Alleghany mountains. This is best illustrated by the statement that it has not less than 10,000 miles of navigable tributaries.

Efforts at protection from overflow by means of levees date from the earliest settlements, and have been continued with varying success to the present time.

In 1717 a levee was built to protect the city of New Orleans from overflow. In 1735 De Pratz says that "the levee extended from English Bend, twelve miles below, to thirty miles above and on both sides of the river."

In 1743 an ordinance was promulgated "requiring the inhabitants to complete their levees by the 1st of

January, 1744, under a penalty of forfeiture of their lands to the crown." By the year 1858 nearly the entire alluvial basin from Cairo to the Gulf was leveed.

Between 1861 and 1866 much of this work was lost by neglect and the ravages of war, but to-day there are 1,100 miles of levees. Since 1866 the State and levee districts of Louisiana have expended $15,255,327.13; since 1882 the Mississippi levee districts have expended $3,098,745.74, and Arkansas has expended $340,417.

The States being forbidden by the constitution from making compacts or agreements among themselves, there is no means by which the work of levee building can be prosecuted systematically and scientifically, and each community has to look out for itself. But the levees, such as they are, have furnished a large measure of protection. "In 1882 the total number of crevasses in the levees was 284, aggregating 56.09 miles in width; in 1883 the number of crevasses was 224, with an aggregate width of 34.1 miles; in 1884 the crevasses numbered 204, aggregating 10.64 miles in width." They caused a general overflow.

In the flood of 1890, which in height exceeded and in duration equalled any of which we have record, the total number of crevasses in the whole 1,100 miles of levees was but 23, aggregating but 4¼ miles in width, and notwithstanding the sensational accounts to the contrary, fully 80 per cent. of the alluvial basin enjoyed absolute immunity from the floods. Without these levees, the entire basin, excepting possibly a few high ridges of limited area, would be uninhabitable. That it is entirely practicable to protect the whole valley by levees is demonstrated by these facts and attested by the outspoken opinions of all engineers who have studied the subject. It is estimated that $10,000,000 furnished by the government, added to what the people of the valley would contribute, would suffice to accomplish this result. This Delta embraces about 40,000 square miles, of which at least 36,000, or 23,000,000 of acres can be reclaimed and placed in cultivation. The value of these lands when protected from overflow would easily reach $30 per acre, or a total of $690,000,000. We hold that it is the duty of the government to come to the rescue, and make the conquest of the Mississippi valley complete. Until this is done, the world will not have reaped the full harvest sown by Hernando De Soto when he discovered the Mississippi in April, 1541.

The river, though now put in active competition with railroads, remains an important factor in the transportation system of the country, and in the near future will be esteemed as highly by the inhabitants of the Western States as it was by the early settlers, who threatened Spain with war that they might enjoy its benefits.

In 1887 the rate on grain per 100 pounds by rail from St. Louis to New York was 32 2-15 cents. By river via New Orleans it was by steamboats 18¼ cents and by barges but 6 cents. Here there is room for a saving of 14 and 26 2-15 cents respectively per 100 pounds. Speaking upon this point, Mr. Frank Gaienne, president of the St. Louis Merchants' Exchange, said: "The improvement of the

Mississippi and the consequent increase of trade to the seaboard by the reduction of rates by the river route, compelled the trunk lines to meet the river rate. The value of this reduced rate to the farmers in wheat alone, from 1881 to 1885, taking the route to New York and New Orleans, was on the average 6 cents per bushel. At the estimate of the Agricultural Department for 1885, which was 357,112,000 bushels, a saving of 6 cents on that amount of grain means $21,166,720 more money in the hands of the farmers, to say nothing of the benefits to all other kinds of business."

Sharp competition has sprung up latterly between the grain growers of the West and those of the Baltic, the Indies and Russia. The exportation of grain from these countries has grown so enormously within the past few years as to displace large quantities from America, which before found a market in Europe. The cheapness of transportation offered by the Mississippi furnishes the only hope to them of being able to meet this rivalry with profit. The value of shipments passing through the Sault St. Marie in 1889 is estimated at about $83,000,000. Captain J. W. Bryant, of New Orleans, stated before the House Committee on Rivers and Harbors recently that for the same year, as taken by him directly from the manifests of vessels, the value of shipments arriving at and departing from the port of New Orleans was upwards of $90,000,000.

Thus, it will be seen that the river is, even in its comparatively unimproved condition, a gigantic commercial factor.

The construction of the jetties by Captain James B. Eads has made New Orleans a harbor of the first-class by providing ample depth at the entrance to the river from the gulf. But there is much yet to be done by the government before the capability of the river as a servant of the great and growing commerce of the country can be fully utilized.

The work needed is elaborated in the annual reports of the Mississippi River commission, which was created in 1879 for the especial purpose of improving the river.

To secure the needed appropriations it is only necessary that the people of the United States shall have their attention intelligently directed to the subject.

EARLY EFFORTS FOR NATIONAL RECOGNITION, CULMINATING IN THE BUILDING OF THE EADS JETTIES.

"In considering the Mississippi river, we must regard it as a river of sand as well as of water." In the foregoing sentence, Hon. Randall Lee Gibson, United States Senator from Louisiana, pithily stated the problem which it has been the endeavor of civil and military engineers to solve for three-quarters of a century. This problem presents phenomena seemingly discordant and irreconcilable, and yet known to be controlled by and obedient to fixed laws. To obtain accurate knowledge of these laws was the first essential step toward the perfection of a plan that should overcome all difficulties and keep this mighty stream under human control.

The first official action by the general government in this direction was taken in 1822, when two engineer officers of the army, General S. Bernard and J. G. Totten, after a careful study of the river, made an elaborate report (December 22, 1822) in which they set forth the result of their investigations, and declared: "The only means which appear practicable to us is the construction of dikes. They operate by diminishing the current above them, thus economizing the expanse of water, at the same time constraining the current to rush with greater velocity through the narrow space to be deepened."

In the same report they describe the effects of the floods they had witnessed, saying: "While the waters of this river are over its banks, the operation of the current being in proportion to its elevation and consequent increase of velocity, the changes which are produced in the bed of the river are great, sudden and numerous. Then are produced those multiplied turns and elbows which so strikingly characterize this great river, and which increase its channel to the double what it would have been if the banks could have resisted its current. The corresponding concave parts of these turns are sometimes separated only by a very narrow neck, which being cut through by the waters, as often happens, present a new and navigable channel of perhaps a half mile in length, in lieu of the old one of 15 or 20 miles. The abandoned channel is entirely divided from the river except in floods, and on the west side, especially, becomes a lake."

The floods of the Mississippi are one of the phenomena to be understood that they may be regulated. The other is the low-water periods. "At certain seasons of the year," said Senator Gibson, in one of his instructive speeches, "the water subsides, the channel is blocked by snags and sandbars, and for a great distance there is only from four to eight and a-half feet depth. This condition continues not for a few days or a few weeks, but for several months during every year, interrupting trade and commerce, and making its navigation difficult and perilous ; the largest and costliest boats, in which great sums are invested, and that give employment to thousands of people, are compelled to lie idle; the navigation of the river is almost as effectually closed as if artificial dams were built across its bed."

While the report made in 1822 by army engineers awakened much interest in the improvement in the Mississippi, and was probably the primary movement which ultimately led to the large grant of public lands made in 1840, yet there was not at that time any popular comprehension of the importance of the work needed, or of the vast national interests that would be served if it were undertaken and accomplished. In 1845, two distinguished Congressmen, James Gadsen and James Guthrie, acting as a sub-committee, made as thorough an examination of the subject as was possible, and prepared a report upon the navigation of the Mississippi, which was approved by Hon. John C. Calhoun, who submitted it to Congress. In that report the situation was carefully stated, and it was said:

"The expenditures on the Mississippi thus far, if reports are to be credited, have produced no results corresponding to the vast sums appropriated. When the channel has been straightened at one point it has been lengthened at another, and obstructions or deposits in one bend have only been transferred in their removal to another. 'Sawyers' and 'planters' have in one season been reduced in number to be replaced by the succeeding one.

"The only fact clearly established, and it is one to which attention should be particularly directed as bearing with peculiar influence on the proposition submitted, is that where the banks of the Mississippi have been leveed and prevented from inundating the swamps, the spring rises are scarcely perceptible, and the surplus waters are discharged by deepening the bed; its currents no longer able to rise and expand over a wider surface, they have to deepen the bed to furnish vent for the waters to be discharged. The reclaiming, therefore, the swamps and confining the river to its bed will deepen it, and do more to preserve unimpaired the navigation of the Mississippi than all the projects which have hitherto been devised or acted on for its improvement. The suggestion, however, is worthy of examination, and it is the stronger recommended as it may accomplish a great object at comparatively little cost. The swamps of the Mississippi now worthless, and made so by the inundations of the that river, may be made, by their own reclamation, the instruments of improving the navigation of that stream."

In this declaration is shown the fact that although the work of the preceding years had been so disconnected that what was done at one point had destroyed the work at some other, still the theory advanced by Engineers Bernard and Totten seems to have been proved correct.

At great cost the country was gradually acquiring knowledge as to how to deal with this "river of sand as well as of water." It was also slowly, very slowly indeed, beginning to learn that the great waterway that extended from Canada to the Gulf was a national stream, beyond the power of the interior States to improve and to control. In his last speech in Congress Henry Clay, the greatest of the distinguished galaxy of statesmen that adorned that era, referred to this public ignorance, or narrowness of view, with a pathós all the more impressive, because of his broad national ideas and his prolonged and eminent services to his country. The bill making appropriations for river and harbor improvements being before the Senate, Mr. Clay, after some preliminary remarks, said :

"An honorable senator has gotten up and told us that here is an appropriation of $2,300,000. With regard to the appropriations made for that portion of the country from which I come, the great valley of the Mississippi, I will say that we are a persevering people, a feeling people and a contrasting people; and how long will it be before the people of this vast valley will rise *en masse* and tumble down your little hair-splitting distinctions about what is national, and demand what is just and fair on the part of this government in relation to their great interests? The Mississippi, with all its tributaries, constitute a part of a great system, and if the system be not national I should like to know one that is national. We are told that a little work, great in its value, one for which I shall vote with great pleasure—the breakwater in the little State of Delaware—is a great national work, while a work which has for its object the improvement of that vast system of rivers which constitute the valley of the Mississippi, which is to save millions and millions of property and many human lives, is not a work to be done because not national!

Around the region of the coast of the Atlantic, the Mexican Gulf and the Pacific coast everywhere we pour out in boundless and unmeasured streams the treasure of the United States, but none to the interior of the West, the valley of the Mississippi. Every cent is contested and denied for that object.

Sir, I call upon the Northwestern Senators, upon Western Senators, upon Eastern Senators, upon Senators from all quarters of the Union, to recollect that we are part of our common country."

Had the facilities for the transmission of congressional proceedings been then what they are now, this address would have appeared in full in every morning paper in the land, and this appeal would have been responded to by the devoted friends of Henry Clay in every State. But it was heard only by his audience in the Senate chamber, and was then buried in the pages of the Congressional Record. It had its effect, however, upon pending legislation, for an appropriation for work on the Mississippi was made.

In 1850 Colonel Humphrey and Captain Abbot, of the United States Engineers, were detailed to make a complete survey of the Mississippi. They spent ten years in the work. Their report has been pronounced "a monument of industry and learning." It convinced many, in and out of Congress, that some continuous system out to be adopted for insuring the commerce of the river against the losses consequent upon floods and low water periods. The general opinion seems to have been that more levees should be built, and that those already constructed should be strengthened where necessary. Special committees were created by Congress, who agreed upon a bill for constructing levees, which passed one house only to be lost in the other. Meanwhile, the people of the Mississippi delta were steadily taxing themselves to maintain the existing barriers, which were essential to their protection. Then came the war, with its attendant devastation. During its continuance the levees were neglected, and many were either in part or wholly destroyed. Soon after peace was declared, in 1865, Secretary Stanton ordered the levees to be rebuilt, believing, says Senator Gibson, that it was an "act of humanity to restore these public works essential to the good order of society, and now needed more than ever by a people struggling with poverty amid social and political conditions involving a disruption of traditions and customs and established relations, but it was not done."

In 1874 a commission was again appointed to determine what ought to be done. President Grant was strongly in favor of its recommendations to reconstruct the levees, but even his influence was not sufficiently powerful to produce favorable action in Congress.

Meanwhile a new interest in the condition and needs of the lower Mississippi valley had been created that was to have a most potential influence upon its future.

Population had followed the lines of the trans-continental railroads and their feeders until great States had been carved out of the country on both sides of the Rocky mountains; prosperous cities had sprung into existence; vast areas of wilderness had been brought under cultivation, and for their immense crops of wheat and corn there was no adequate transportation. From all these fertile farms and prosperous cities came a demand for the improvement of the Mississippi. The plan of a voluntary association was suggested. St. Louis took the lead in this matter, and soon a powerful organization was effected, numbering in its membership many influential citizens of every State from Minnesota to Louisiana, and conventions were held, statistics were compiled, public spirit was aroused, and the public opinion of the entire region from Canada to the gulf was brought to bear upon Congress. The first tangible result of this spontaneous uprising was the organization in the House of Representatives of the forty-fourth Congress of a permanent committee on levees, the first of the kind that had ever been created. This committee framed a bill for the rebuilding of the levees and for the protection of the entire alluvial region from floods, but although it was earnestly and ably advocated it failed to get a third of the votes of the House. The great West was determined that something should be done. At least the mouth of the Mississippi should be made an open gateway to the sea. Capt. James B. Eads, an eminent civil engineer of St. Louis, devised a plan for the accomplishment of this work, which was pressed upon and carried through Congress. The task was entrusted to the man whose genius had devised the plan, and he carried it through to a triumphant success. At last the nation recognized in some measure the importance of the Mississippi river as a highway of commerce.

PASSAGE OF THE BILL CREATING THE COMMISSION—THE EADS PLAN.

When the plan proposed by Captain Eads for making a permanent ship channel at the mouth of the Mississippi was first proposed, there were many engineers of eminence who doubted its feasibility, and some of them spent much time and labor in arguing against it. But after the great work had been accomplished and all that its ingenious inventor had promised had been more than fulfilled, the people of the upper as well as the lower valley were inspired with greater confidence than ever that human skill was equal to the task of confining the Mississippi within bounds that it should never pass, to the great advantage of commerce, and to the reasonable security of life and property throughout all the extensive region subject to frequent overflows.

If this could be accomplished there was every reason why it should be undertaken at once, for the rapid growth of the Northwest and the consequent increase of its grain crops made more and cheaper transportation facilities an imperative necessity. From the head of navigation to Port Eads this was the dominant subject of thought and discussion among the people. "The wisdom of Congress should be invoked," said General

Garfield, "to devise some plan by which the great river shall cease to be a terror to those who dwell upon its banks, and by which its shipping may safely carry the industrial products of 25,000,000 of people." The people, by popular petitions, by memorials from chambers of commerce and boards of trade, by resolutions passed by the State legislatures, did invoke the wisdom of the Forty-fourth Congress. A measure was introduced in that body April 26, 1876, authorizing the President to appoint a commission to improve the Mississippi river. This was referred to the committee on commerce, which invited Captain Eads to present his views as to the proper course to be pursued. That distinguished civil engineer had long been convinced that the conditions that existed at the mouth of the river prevailed throughout its entire length. In a pamphlet published by him in 1874 he stated that the chief portion of the sediment discharged by the river into the Gulf is carried in suspension, and "that the amount of this matter and the size and weight of the particles which the stream is enabled to hold up and carry forward depend wholly upon the rapidity of the stream, modified, however, by its depth." Later, in his review of Humphrey's and Abbott's report on the physics and hydraulics of the Mississippi, he argued on this basis, showing the relation between the current and the suspended sediment, and then demonstrating the practicability of deepening the river and lowering the floods without the use of waste weirs or outlets. Following the same line of argument before the committee, "he held that by applying the jetty system to the river, confining its waters in their highest stages and contracting the channel where unduly wide and protecting the banks against caving, works wholly practicable and inexpensive, a uniform channel might be obtained affording deep water all the year round for the largest vessels to St. Louis, and at the same time and by the same means the slope or flood surface would be so lowered as to prevent destructive floods—floods destructive not only to commerce and trade and the vehicles of transportation, to life and property on the river, but destructive of all government, of all industry, of the property, the earnings, the schools, the churches, the very existence of organized society throughout the wide alluvial region."

In concluding his exhaustive argument Captain Eads said:

"There can be no doubt of the entire feasibility of so correcting the Mississippi river from Cairo to the Gulf that a channel depth of 20 feet during the low-water seasons can be permanently secured throughout its entire course, and that the alluvial lands on each side of its waters can be made absolutely safe from overflow without levees by such correction. This can be accomplished for a sum entirely within the ability of the government, and one really insignificant when compared with the benefits which would flow from such improvement.

"Until such work is accomplished, an annual expenditure for the maintenance of the levees is imperative."

It is proper to say that there were some distinguished civil and military engineers, as well as some steamship captains and others doing business on the Mississippi, who held contrary opinions and argued against those of Captain Eads with much earnestness and plausibility. But his views continued to gain ground the more they were criticised, and the emphatic declaration with which he concluded undoubtedly led Congress eventually to enact the law establishing the Mississippi River Commission.

The Forty-fifth Congress, early in its session, enlarged the scope of the committee on levees by adding to its title "and improvements of the Mississippi River," thus enabling it to take jurisdiction of all legislation on these subjects. Many measures were introduced and referred to this committee, which finally framed a substitute for them all, entitled, "a bill to provide for the organization of the Mississippi river improvement commission, and for the correction, permanent location, and deepening of the channel and improvement of the navigation of said river and the protection of its alluvial lands." This substitute was submitted to the House by Hon. E. W. Robertson, of Louisiana, to whose profound knowledge on this subject is due the framing and submission of this important measure.

There were many in and out of Congress who were willing that whatever money was necessary should be appropriated for improving the commerce of the stream, who were at the same time opposed to any expenditures for the protection of the alluvial lands. The idea was industriously circulated by the opponents of all measures for improving the Mississippi river, that this bill was an attempt in disguise to recover and give value to immense areas of land belonging to private owners, and these insidious attacks had unquestionably considerable effect upon people who lived in other sections remote from the valley, and were unacquainted with its condition and needs. Two Massachusetts representatives, Messrs. Robinson and Banks, each, in advocating the commission bill, explained the necessity for the proposed action. Mr. Robinson said:

"The committee have found these two subjects to be interdependent. They have not seen in the investigation they have given that the one necessarily stands apart from the other. All the writers and all the engineers from whom they have heard declare that in some measure, greater or less, the protection of the lands has also an influence upon the navigable character of the river. * * This bill is intended to provide a commission to devise a plan for the improvement of the Mississippi river and the protection of the alluvial lands combined. If as a part of the whole plan for the improvement of the river for the purposes of navigation, and incidental thereto, the lands of the valley may be protected, I am in favor of it."

General Banks, whose campaigns on the lower Mississippi and its tributaries had familiarized him with its conditions and needs, supported the bill ardently, and with patriotic breadth characteristic of that statesman, he said:

"I have already stated that the improvement of the alluvial lands is incidental to this work. It cannot be separated from it. No declaration or act of Congress can prevent it. If we make the river what it ought to be we will make 40,000,000 acres of the best cotton and sugar lands on the face of the earth in consequence of the necessary improvement of the river—40,000,000 where now only 1,000,000 exists. It is inseparable from it and incidental to the improvement of the river."

Hon. Randall L. Gibson, then a representative, but now a senator from Louisiana, who from the beginning has been one of the most intelligent and indefatigable advocates of Mississippi river improvement, said:

"A jetty is a levee, in the popular sense of the word, within the bed or channel of the river, while a levee is a jetty on the bank of the stream. This plan rests upon the theory that in sedimentary rivers, in the Mississippi particularly, as the water is confined its velocity and depth is increased and the surface lowered, and that thus two great objects may be accomplished by one and the same method, namely, 'ease and safety' to navigation and protection to the industrious people on the banks from the dreaded floods."

But notwithstanding the earnestness of the friends of the measure, and the unanswerable arguments urged in its favor, the bill failed.

At the extra session of the Forty-sixth Congress several new bills were modeled on that which failed, but limiting the field of work. These were followed by one prepared by Representative Gibson, of Louisiana, introduced May 10, 1879, entitled "a bill to provide for the appointment of a 'Mississippi River Commission' for the improvement of said river from the head of the passes near its mouth to its head-waters." This measure was sent to the committee, was favorably reported back to the House, which passed it the first week in June, with but twenty votes against it. In the Senate it was amended in some unimportant particulars and then passed with but four adverse votes. The House accepted the Senate amendments, the bill was sent to the President, and was approved June 28, 1879. The following is a verbatim copy of this important measure:

[PUBLIC—No. 34.]

"An Act to Provide for the Appointment of a 'Mississippi River Commission' for the Improvement of Said River from the Head of the Passes near its Mouth to its Head-waters.

Be it enacted by the Senate and House of Representatives of the United States of America in Congress assembled, That a commission is hereby created, to be called 'The Mississippi River Commission,' to consist of seven members.

Sec. 2. The President of the United States shall, by and with the consent of the Senate, appoint seven commissioners, three of whom shall be selected from the Engineer Corps of the Army, one from the Coast and Geodetic Survey, and three from civil life, two of whom shall be civil engineers. And any vacancy which may occur in the commission shall in like manner be filled by the President of the United States; and he shall designate one of the commissioners appointed from the Engineer Corps of the Army to be president of the commission. The commissioners appointed from the Engineer Corps of the Army and the Coast and Geodetic Survey shall receive no other pay or compensation than is now allowed them by law, and the other three commissioners shall receive as pay and compensation for their services each the sum of $3,000 per annum; and the commissioners appointed under this act shall remain in office subject to removal by the President of the United States.

Sec. 3. It shall be the duty of said commission to direct and complete such surveys of said river, between the Head of the Passes near its mouth to its headwaters as may now be in progress, and to make such additional surveys, examinations and investigations, topographical, hydrographical and hydrometrical, of said river and its tributaries, as may be deemed necessary by said commission to carry out the objects of this act. And to enable said commission to complete such surveys, examinations and investigations, the Secretary of War shall, when requested by said commission, detail from the Engineer Corps of the Army such officers and men as may be necessary, and shall place in the charge and for the use of said commission such vessel or vessels and such machinery and instruments as may be under his control and may be deemed necessary. And the Secretary of the Treasury shall, when requested by said commission, in like manner detail from the Coast and Geodetic

Survey such officers and men as may be necessary, and shall place in the charge and for the use of said commission such vessel or vessels and such machinery and instruments as may be under his control and may be deemed necessary. And the said commission may, with the approval of the Secretary of War, employ such additional force and assistants, and provide, by purchase or otherwise, such vessels or boats and such instruments and means as may be deemed necessary.

Sec. 4. It shall be the duty of said commission to take into consideration and mature such plan or plans and estimates as will correct, permanently locate and deepen the channel and protect the banks of the Mississippi river; improve and give safety and ease to the navigation thereof; prevent destructive floods; promote and facilitate commerce, trade and the postal service; and when so prepared and matured, to submit to the Secretary of War a full and detailed report of their proceedings and actions, and of such plans, with estimates of the cost thereof, for the purpose aforesaid, to be by him transmitted to Congress; provided that the commission shall report in full upon the practicability, feasibility and probable cost of the various plans known as the jetty system, the levee system and the outlet system, as well as upon such others as they deem necessary.

Sec. 5. The said commission may, prior to the completion of all the surveys and examinations contemplated by this act, prepare and submit to the Secretary of War plans, specifications and estimates of costs for such immediate works as, in the judgment of said commission, may constitute a part of the general system of works herein contemplated, to be by him transmitted to Congress.

Sec. 6. The Secretary of War may detail from the Engineer Corps of the Army of the United States an officer to act as secretary of said commission.

Sec. 7. The Secretary of War is hereby authorized to expend the sum of $175,000, or so much thereof as may be necessary, for the payment of the salaries herein provided for, and of the necessary expenses incurred in the completion of such surveys as may now be in progress, and of such additional surveys, examinations and investigations as may be deemed necessary, reporting the plans and estimates, and the plans, specifications and estimates contemplated by this act, as herein provided for; and said sum is hereby appropriated for said purposes out of any money in the treasury not otherwise appropriated.

Approved June 28, 1879."

When the amended bill reached the House from the Senate and was called up for final consideration, Mr. Gibson briefly explained its scope and purposes. After describing how at certain seasons sand bars and snags close the navigation of the river, and how at other seasons the river becomes a mighty roaring torrent, destructive not only to human life and property, but destructive to the commerce and trade upon its waters ; and how these floods cause such changes of the channel itself as to threaten the isolation of such thriving cities as Vicksburg and Natchez, that have become what they are because they are river ports; and after referring to the immense losses by destruction of steamers and barges, in which the commerce of the river is floated, and to the frequent wrecking of large and small craft by these floods, Mr. Gibson says:

"At night and in storms there is absolutely no protection. It is estimated that these extraordinary perils impose a tax of not less than $10,000,000 annually on the increased rates of insurance alone. We know what the difficulties are. They have been surveyed and reports made of them to Congress. But no complete and comprehensive system for their removal has been submitted to this House or to the country.

"This commission is created with the hope that they may devise some plan, economical, feasible, and complete, that shall give us deep water at all seasons of the year, and prevent these destructive floods, so ruinous, not only to the country through which it flows, but to the mighty commerce that carries the productions of the teeming millions who inhabit the great valley to the market of the world and brings back in exchange the wealth of other countries.

"Mr. Speaker, I do not, I can not, believe any gentleman will be disposed to vote against reasonable and just appropriations for wing-dams, jetties, and levees, should this commission, after a thorough and scientific examination of the subject, report that these are the appropriate and necessary instrumentalities to deepen and correct the channel, to prevent destructive floods, to afford safety and ease to navigation, and facilities to trade and commerce upon our great inland sea; that they are, in fact, to the Mississippi river what water-gaps, sheltering piers and harbors, and lighthouses and beacons and buoys are to the sea and lake coasts.

"Would you decline such appropriations so clearly constitutional under the power to regulate commerce, when they are smaller in proportion to the commercial interest at stake than upon the ocean or the like, because at the same time they would protect the hard-working and industrious people in the mighty valley against overflows, or because they would reclaim the most productive region on this continent and secure to it an intelligent, vigorous population to develop its inexhaustible resources and contribute to the strength and glory of our country."

MANNER AND EXTENT OF THE WORK DONE UNDER THE SUPERVISION OF THE MISSISSIPPI RIVER COMMISSION.

The preliminary report noticed in the preceding chapter was followed January 8, 1881, by a statement of the progress made by the commission in surveys, observations and examinations, together with others of a preliminary nature concerning the upper Mississippi, from the Falls of St. Anthony to the mouth of the Illinois river, and upon the proposed reservoir system. To these were appended the report of a special comcommittee of the commission on the subject of outlets and levees on the lower river. While in the main report and its appendixes there was necessarily much theorizing and speculative argument, because the time had been insufficient for the collection of all the data upon which accurate conclusions could be based, still there had been a sufficient number of facts ascertained to enable the commission to recommend a continuance of the work on the upper Mississippi on the plan employed by the army engineers, and to increase confidence in the practicability of the system of work proposed in the first preliminary report for improving the lower Mississippi. It was made clearly apparent in these several reports that Congress had undertaken a work that would require a long time and a large expenditure to complete, and that true economy required that as far as possible the work should be continued without interruption to a finish, and that in places where this could not be done during the high-water periods, the rule should be to construct only so much as would be reasonably certain to resist the effects of floods and remain intact when they subsided. It was shown that the system required for the improvement of the upper river was in many respects unlike that needed for the lower, because of the difference in their natural conditions, but that, notwithstanding these differences, it was essential that the improvement of the entire stream, from its head-waters to its mouth, should be under one supervision in order to insure unity of plan, economic work and a successful outcome.

That Congress appreciated to some extent, at least, the importance of the work and had confidence in the wisdom of the plans of procedure adopted by the commission was manifested by the appropriation of $1,000,000. (Act of March 3, 1881.) As the work advanced and its good results became more and more apparent, Congress continued to make specific appropriations until the sum total of these and of unexpended balances of appropriations for local works which were transferred to the commission's account from March 3, 1881, to August 11, 1888, amounted to $13,381,581.77. Of this large sum there remained to the credit of the commission at the close of the fiscal year, June 30,

1890, a balance of $375,618.34. The expenditures during the nine years were:

For river works.................... $9,759,217.89
For levees......................... 3,183,745.54

Total.......... ....$12,942,963.43

This large outlay includes, however, the cost of the extensive plant which it was necessary to create at a cost of $1,500,000 for the prosecution of the work. This consists of steamers, barges, a great variety of machinery and utensils, none of which, except for the usual expenditures on account of wear and breakage of tools, will need to be renewed during the further progress of the work.

"In addition to the cost of the plant considerable money was expended in the first year or two of the commission's existence in experiments. It was necessary to put theories into practice to test their value. The commission wisely followed Davy Crockett's famous motto, "Be sure you are right, then go ahead." To have done otherwise might have caused so great a waste of money upon valueless works that the country, wearying of such futile efforts, might have insisted upon the abolition of the commission, and the abandonment of all further attempts to control the river. But when investigations and experiments had shown conclusively what were the right things to do, a system was adopted and followed that has accomplished far more than many advocates of the commission dared to expect, and which bids fair, when the work shall be finished, to justify the faith of the late Captain Eads in 'the entire feasibility of so correcting the Mississippi from Cairo to the Gulf that a channel depth of 20 feet during low-water seasons can be permanently secured throughout its entire course, and that the alluvial lands on each side of its waters can be made absolutely safe from overflow.'

"This system consisted of three classes, viz: levee repairs and construction; revetments for the protection of caving banks; and contraction works, which consist of the construction of preamble dikes in certain places designed for the immediate local deepening of the channel for the benefit of navigation. In his testimony before the Senate committee on the improvement of the Mississippi river May 21, 1888, Captain S. S. Leach, U. S. A., gave the following description of the methods of levee construction:

"The line of the levee is located from various considerations that affect it, but we try to get it on the highest ground, so as to make the least height of embankment. It also must not come too near the river, and it must not go too far away from the river, because that makes it too high. You want to get as near the river as possible to be on the high ground, but you must not get too near, or it will be caved in shortly. When the line is determined, a swath 200 feet wide is cleared, and about in the middle of that swath an interior line, equal in width to the base of the levee, is thoroughly cleared of all surface vegetable matter, leaves and everything of that sort. Near one side of the crown of the levee, say 3 feet from the centre-line of the levee, on the river side, a ditch is dug which is 2 feet wide on top, 1 foot at the bottom and 3 feet deep. That ditch is excavated, and then a clear, fresh sub-soil, which does not contain any roots, is put into the ditch and packed. This is generally done by a boy on a mule, riding up and down the ditch until the mule will scarcely make a print. This ditch, being thoroughly tramped, cuts off any possibility of the water soaking through the ground under the levee in any quantity that would be dangerous; and any continuous root-channels, and particularly the burrowing of animals, will be cut off by this ditch. The embankment is then begun and carried up to the necessary height, the standard height in the upper part of the river being 3 feet above the highest known water. The slopes are usually $3\frac{1}{2}$ on each side to 1, and the crown is generally about equal to the height. So you may say that the base covered by a levee is 8 times the height, 7 times in two slopes and once in the crown, practically 8 times; so that an 8-foot levee will cover 64 feet of ground.

"This levee is constructed in a very solid manner. Great care is taken that all parts of it shall be clean, and it must be carried out regularly from the slopes in uniform layers, so as to get perfect compactness and uniform settlement. When it is done with barrows, it is carried one-fifth of its height above the true grade, to allow for settlement. If it is done with teams, which of course pack it very much closer, it is not necessary to carry it so high. That is to say, for a levee the grade of which is 10 feet high, the barrow work is carried up to 12 feet, with the expectation that it will settle 2 feet. Team work we put up to 11 feet or above.

The surface of the levee, after it is finished, is dressed and sodded with Bermuda grass, which affords a very tough sod, and prevents a heavy wash. It runs very rapidly, and lives longer than any known grass under the water, so that there is less probability of killing the grass while the water is above it."

Revetment and dike works have been scarcely more than begun. These have been appropriately defined, the first as defensive, the second as aggressive works. The purpose of a revetment is to stop banks from caving. To do this a mat is woven of green, flexible willow shoots. The process of making it and placing it in position was described by Captain Leach to the Senate committee as follows:

"The mattress is woven continuously. We have a barge on the river with a loom, as it may be called, on it. We weave the width of the barge, and then let the barge slip out until the woven edge comes down to the front edge of the barge, and then weave on another shift, and slide that off, and so on, going down the river as far as the slope of the bank, the strength of the current and other circumstances of construction will permit. The lengths usually woven, speaking generally, are not far from 900 to 1,100 feet. When that is done the mat is thoroughly bound together with cables so as to make it sufficiently strong. Barges are brought along the outside, and men with wheelbarrows haul stone on and deposit it uniformly just as long as they are able to go on with a loaded barrow. In other words, they destroy as much of the floatation as can possibly be done. Then some stone is carried on board at the head and thrown on the head of the mat, which is held up from the barge by ropes. When a superabundant weight is on the mat the ropes from the barge are slackened, and it sinks four or five feet below the surface. The sunken portion extends only 100 feet or so down the stream; that leaves a little space of clear water, and in that water we float in loaded barges. They are fastened to the mooring barge at the head of the mat by lines at each end, and skilled linesmen are placed at the ends to slacken off the lines when everything is ready. A gang of men is placed along the side of the barge, and as they are dropped down they keep throwing stone off, and the head of the mat being lowered to the bottom at the same time, the whole structure is swept down to the bottom."

The slope of the caving bank is covered in the same manner up to high-water mark. The silt suspended in the flowing current is caught in the interstices of these mats, soon filling them compactly, and creating a solid wall, which finds a support on the tough clay layers, of which the banks in part consist, and, "being held in place by them, it in turn holds the sand layers in place."

The dike or aggressive works are local in their position and effect, but are general in their benefits.

They are designed to afford greater depth of water for navigation, but they have no immediate relation to the bringing of the river under permanent and complete control. "They are formed," said Captain Leach, "by driving piles at intervals in the bed of the river and connecting them strongly by timbers and iron ties, etc., to give them the requisite strength to resist the onset of the current, of ice and of drifts. They are run out from the bank in parallel directions, a system of them beginning with a short one at the upper end, followed about four or five or six or seven hundred feet down by one extending a little farther out, and so on down until the last one is reached, which extends out to about where the corrected channel is designed to be." Their action is to silt up large areas of the present bed, forcing the water to flow through a narrower low-water bed than it naturally would do—forcing it to remain in a single channel, and to scour out the four or five feet depths to ten or twelve feet, or as much more as can be obtained.

Of the good results that have accrued from these various classes of work there is voluminous evidence. Rivermen whose business has made them familiarly acquainted with the Mississippi for many years are now warm and cordial supporters of the commission, although when it was created ten years ago their feelings towards it were the reverse of friendly. In March, 1868, the Pilots' Benevolent & Improvement Society, whose members reside in St. Louis, Pittsburgh, Cincinnati, Evansville, Cairo, Memphis, Vicksburg and New Orleans, passed unanimously the following resolution at a meeting held in St. Louis, and forwarded an attested copy thereof to the chairman of the River and Harbor Committee of Congress:

"*Resolved*, That we, as a body, emphatically indorse the past workings of the Mississippi River Commission in the improvement of the Mississippi river, and base our decision on our every-day observation of the work and its beneficial effect in deepening the channel of the river."

The merchants of Memphis, Tenn., realizing the great danger threatening their business interests because of the caving of the banks on their water front, raised the sum of $60,000 by subscription, and expended it upon works similar to those of the commission, and succeeded in converting the caving bluff into a solid wall which has stood the assaults of two large floods without impairment. This was a more practical expression of approval than the resolution of the pilots.

The most recent, and perhaps the most convincing testimony of any on record, appears in the report submitted April 30, 1890, to the Mississippi River and Levee Improvement Convention, by a committee of 14 engineers, to whom had been assigned the duty of preparing a statement on the subject of levees. The great flood of last spring was slowly subsiding when this convention, comprising influential delegates from 7 Mississippi river States, assembled to consider the situation. The report submitted by their committee of engineers contained the following statistics:

In 1882 the total number of crevasses in the levees

was 284, aggregating 56 9-10 miles in width. In 1883 the number of crevasses was 225, with an aggregate width of 34 and 1-100 miles. In 1884 the crevasses numbered 204, aggregating 106 and 4-100 miles in width.

The result of the crevasses enumerated during these three years was a general overflow of the Mississippi Delta. In the present flood, the dangers of which are nearly passed, the crevasses which have occurred number 23, aggregating about 4¼ miles in width, in a total length of 1,100 miles of levees, one-half of one per cent. of the total lines of levees, notwithstanding that the present flood has exceeded those of the three years cited in the height attained at Memphis and all points below and has not been exceeded in duration.

This excess of height was: at Memphis 0.5 feet, at Helena 0.6 feet, at Sunflower landing 1.2 feet, at Arkansas City 2.3 feet, at Greenville 1.7 feet, at Providence 3.1 feet, at Vicksburg 0.1 feet, at Natchez 0.8 feet and at New Orleans 0.5 feet. The general result has been a large measure of protection afforded by the levees this year, notwithstanding the extraordinary character of flood, which has never been enjoyed during previous high waters of considerable magnitude. For example, in the Yazoo basin between 80 and 85 per cent. of its area is protected from overflow, there being only one crevasse of 280 feet width affecting a very small area. In 180 miles of levees, extending from the upper extreme southward, there were other crevasses on this front below that locality. On the

Tensas front are two reaches of continuous levee, being respectively 81 and 125 miles in length.

The right bank below Red river has 180 miles of continuous unbroken levee, and the left bank has 200 miles with only one break. Of the territory dependent upon the last named levees 75 per cent. has been protected. The percentage of areas protected as above noted embraces all classes of land subject to overflow; in the lands for cultivation on the more elevated portions the percentage of lands protected is much greater.

In view of these statistics the committee was justified in declaring "that very great progress has been made during the past five years in the construction of a complete levee system by the joint efforts of the general government and the riparian States, and also that experience of the present flood has strongly added to our conviction that such a system presents the only solution to the problem of the protection of the alluvial valley from inundation in connection with the general improvement of the river."

THE MISSISSIPPI RIVER—WHAT IT NEEDS AND WHY IT NEEDS IT.

[The *Manufacturers' Record* is able to present this week one of the most important and valuable of its series of articles on Mississippi river improvements, from the pen of Capt. Smith S. Leach, United States engineer, now located at Boston, formerly of Memphis. Capt. Leach was for 12 years in active charge of Mississippi river improvements, for 5 years secretary of the Mississippi river commission, and for 7 years United States engineer in charge of government work on the river between Cairo and the mouth of White river. He is regarded by the people of that section as one of the ablest engineers in the army, and by many thought to understand the phenomena of the Mississippi river better than any engineer since the time of Capt. Eads.—Editorial in the *Manufacturers' Record.*]

The popular conception of the Mississippi river is that it is simply a stream of water; that its channel is nothing more than a containing vessel, oblivious of its contents; that its floods are only the spilling out of a portion of the water at times when the vessel is too small for its purpose, and that the remedy for such an overflowing river is the same as for an overflowing tub.

The Mississippi is a stream of water, to be sure, but it is very much more than that. The water carries in suspension a varying but always considerable quantity of sediment. Its channel is a plastic conduit, formed by the river itself, and as sensitive to its demands as a mother to the caress of her child, undergoing incessant changes in response to the moods of the current. These changes, so far as they affect the capacity of the channel to do its work, are of two kinds, one of which makes the bed larger and is beneficial, while the other makes it smaller and is detrimental. Both depend upon the ability of the water, considered as a vehicle, to carry the sediment, considered as its load. The vehicular power of the water is derived solely from the fact that it is in motion, and the best index of this power is the amount of motion as represented in the velocity. Changes which make the channel larger are caused by the moving water taking up material from the bed and carrying it away and are the result of accellerated velocity. Changes which make the channel smaller are caused by a portion of the sediment in suspension being deposited on the bottom and are the result of diminished velocity. The conditions of the problem are so infinitely various that no exact relation has been or can be estabblished between the velocity of flowing water and its sediment-carrying power. But thousands of concordant observations demonstrate that no matter with what velocity the river is flowing, and no matter what amount of sediment it may be carrying, if the velocity be decreased, some of the sediment will be deposited. The converse of the proposition, though equally true in the aggregate, is more subject to exception in individual cases. A man is ever more ready to lay down a burden than to take one up, and can carry a load which he could not lift, and a river may be excused for manifesting a like disposition. Changes unfavorable to the efficiency of the channel being produced with greater facility than those favorable, the general tendency of the river in its natural condition is to deteriorate.

The channel which the river now has is the net result of its present silt-transporting power. Any channel which it may have in the future will be the result of the same cause, the then silt-transporting power, and will be better or worse than the present one accordingly as the silt-moving power of the stream has been increased or diminished by natural agencies or human effort. In all questions of the regimen of this river and of changes in it for the purpose of improvement, the matter of first and paramount importance is the effect upon the velocity. Every scheme advanced, no matter by whom or for what reasons, should be at once subjected to this crucial test and made to stand or fall by the result. Any plan, the result of which is to diminish the velocity throughout a section of the channel, is vicious and the advantages promised by it illusory. Plans which tend to conserve or increase the velocity are beneficial, and any disadvantages which may accompany them will be temporary. The velocity is the unerring touchstone which distinguishes the true metal of every applicant for favor, which discovers an enemy in the flattering and boastful outlet, and discloses a friend in the conservative and commonplace levee.

The escape of water from the channel of the river at any point or under any circumstances is accompanied by a reduction of velocity below the point of escape, and by deposits in the area of reduced velocity. A steeper slope is required to maintain the discharge through the diminished cross-section, and the increased slope is obtainable only by an increased height of flood surface above the obstruction. Numerous actual measurements in the bed of the river preclude any doubt of the truth of this proposition. They prove that the escape of water from the channel is accompanied by deposits below, which fact granted, the other changes stated follow as consequences of the elementary laws of hydraulics. The results have been published in detail and so widely distributed that persons desiring information can easily obtain them, and those otherwise inclined would not be benefited by their repetition here. One instance, however, of recent occurrence and of momentous significance will be given.

During the last flood a crevasse in the levee at Nita, La., on the east bank, about 60 miles above New Orleans, having a width of 3,000 feet and a depth of 15 feet, was found by actual measurement to have a discharge of 400,000 cubic feet per second, or 30 per cent. of the entire discharge of the river immediately above the crevasse. As the result of this great outlet the depression of flood surface immediately below the break, where there is a permanent gauge, was one and one-half feet, while at New Orleans, 60 miles below, it was only one foot, and at Plaquemine, 50 miles above, this crevasse had no effect at all. This case shows conclusively that even the engineers who have opposed outlets for the reasons above set forth, have conceded entirely too much as to the immediate relief afforded by depression of flood surface, both in its amount and its extent, and have, by their frankness, given unwarranted aid and comfort to the outlet supporters. That outlets must disappoint the expectations of their advocates as to the amount of lowering of flood surface, for a given volume of escape, was noted by the able pioneers in this subject, Generals Humphreys and Abbott. Lacking actual measurements, they supported the proposition by a very ingenious method of indirect proof, which showed in part, but not completely, the futility of outlets as a means of flood relief. In the case of this year, just cited, an actual outlet was in operation, and all the quantities involved were directly measured. It is a gigantic clinic upon an aggrevated case of the outlet plague, and shows that as a means of inoculation against overflows the outlet is a distinct failure. It has long been conceded that nothing in the way of benefits could be looked for from an outlet, except a temporary local depression of flood surface proportionate to the amount of water taken out, and now it appears that this last surviving hope is shattered. The relief afforded is so trifling as compared with the effort and risk of obtaining it, the effect so insignificant as compared with its cause, that if all the evils of outlets were discredited, there would still be no excuse for making them. A mountain in labor to bring forth a mouse does not surpass such a project as an example of fruitless endeavor.

The size and form of the channel are the result of the effort of the stream, the size determining its sufficiency as a flood chain, and the form its usefulness as a route for navigation. That both are defective is not because the energy is lacking, but because it is misdirected. It has already been intimated that less energy is required to prevent a deposit than to remove it after it is made. So, also, it is far easier to maintain a channel once formed than to open a new one. The river has ample energy to maintain a channel of proper navigable depth and discharging capacity if it can be made to work, as every agency should work to the best advantage and without waste of effort. That it does not so work is due to the fact that the discharge and elevation of the surface are momentarily changing, and with them the positions of bank lines and the location and direction of the line of greatest velocity and maximum effort. No sooner is a sufficient channel obtained in one place than the current leaves it to be obliterated by deposits, while the work which would have easily maintained it is wasted in scouring out a new and inferior one, or perhaps dissipated among several. Every mile of the river is a witness to the truth of this proposition, since the places where the thalweg is stable in position are invariably good, and those where it is shifting are invariably bad. No exception to this rule can be found between Cairo and the Gulf.

What nature has failed to do, and what remains for man to accomplish in order to fit the Mississippi river to his wants and uses, is summed up in the one word, *control*. Guide the current as the skilful workman guides his tool, and it will not fail to carve out a channel commensurate in size with the magnificent agency employed and worthy of the greatest of rivers, traversing and draining the most fruitful and prosperous of countries.

The requisite control is to be obtained by a partial reversal of the present relations of the stream and its bed. It has been shown that the channel is the ready servant, the stream the imperious master. The inconstant current seeks a change, and the subservient shore retires before it. In this respect, as regards the sides of the channel, the present relation of master and slave must be reversed. The servile banks must be strengthened and incited to revolt against their tyrant and to impose a like bondage in return. The current, no longer able to shift at will, devotes its energy to scouring out the bottom, working constantly on the same line and always to the best advantage. The stream, acting under such constraint, will mould its channel to the largest attainable size and discharging capacity, and in the form best adapted to the needs of navigation.

Although this is a statement of theories, it may not be amiss to interject a word as to practice. Types of structures have been evolved in the short experience already had, which may be relied upon to do the work expected of them, and which can be constructed at reasonable cost. A caving bank can be protected or a secondary channel closed with as much certainty as pertains to the building of a road or the digging of a canal. Moreover, these structures have been built at a cost which will allow them to be applied to the entire river without exceeding the sum which the city of Manchester proposes to pay for a canal connecting her with deep water in the Mersey.

Control by means of protected banks is complete and sufficient only so long as the river is within its banks. When it rises above their level the control becomes partial and necessarily inadequate. In years of great floods the surface of the water is above the natural bank level from two months at Cairo to six months at New Orleans. Without artificial restraint nearly one-third of the entire discharge of the river at extreme flood takes place outside its proper channel, as was the case in 1882 above Vicksburg and in 1890 above Helena. The proportion decreases as the bank level is approached, but the aggregate loss of volume during a flood period is enormous. It has been shown that the fundamental principle upon which the improvement is based is the *control* of the water *in the channel*. To allow large quantities to escape, reaching at times one-third the whole, does violence to every idea which can possibly be associated with the word *control*. Water flowing in the channel is the agency of improvement, and when any of it escapes a part of the potential goes with it, and a corresponding measure of the improvement is sacrificed. The current is to be guided so as to do the desired work; the more water the more current, and the more current the more work. When the volume is at a maximum the current has its greatest capacity for work, and will then produce results beyond those which it can attain at any other time. To secure the greatest possible improvement of the channel it is necessary that the greatest attainable volume of water be made to flow through the channel. That this condition is not realized when a large volume is escaping over the sides needs but to be stated to be conceded.

The necessary control of the current beyond that produced by the natural banks, reinforced by protective works, is effected by means of artificial embankments placed on the shores, and of sufficient height to restrain the highest floods. Logically they should follow the shape of the banks, and in practice they do so as far as other and controlling conditions permit. Prevention of escape is control in a large measure, and for that purpose levees, as now built, are fully effective, for they limit the escape to the relatively insignificant volume contained between them and the edges of the channel.

The difference between the effect of a given diminution of velocity in producing deposit and that of equal acceleration in producing scour has been noted. The distinction is a very important one, and finds a new application in this connection. It makes possible a great number of the improved channels in other waters, which have been opened by dredging and have then been maintained by the force of a current which had been powerless to excavate them. Deposit is by its nature a gradual operation, requiring time for its accomplishment, and therefore depending on average conditions. Scour is a more sudden phenomenon, and largely depends on maximum conditions. It is a matter of common observation on all silt-bearing streams that deposits decrease rapidly in rate at higher levels and rarely extend above the average flood plane. The velocity, which represents the possibility of scour, increases regularly when under control to the extreme flood level, the increment for the last foot of rise being as great as for any other foot. A mistaken analogy with the depositing action has caused too much weight to be given to the element of time in producing scour, and has given color to the idea that control of high waters might properly cease at some stage below extreme flood. The utmost limit of channel development, which means the greatest measure of improvement, will result from the greatest intensity of the force which creates the channel and from no other cause. That greatest intensity of errosive force will result from the complete restraint of the greatest floods and from no other cause. Great floods recurring at intervals of several years and confined to the bed of the river will create a channel which but for such floods and 'such restraint never could be created. That channel periodically established, the lesser intervening floods will maintain at a size greater than they could themselves have produced, so that the degree of improvement as maintained will depend upon the magnitude of the greatest floods which are controlled and will reach a maximum only when all floods are controlled.

In its natural condition the channel deteriorates. The deterioration must be stopped and a condition of improvement substituted. The cause of the deterioration is the escape of water from the channel. The remedy is to remove the cause, which can only be done by confining the floods. The improvement of the channel is to be effected by the control of the current. The control at all stages, within or above the banks, will be more effective if the floods are restrained. To depend upon channel works alone is to attempt the improvement with the causes of deterioration in full activity, and is as great a waste of effort as to draw a wagon with the brake set. The complete restraint of floods stops the deterioration of the channel, and at the same time develops to the highest possible degree the forces which tend to its betterment. By a happy coincidence the construction of levees realizes a combination of the greatest force for improvement and the least resistance to its action. That larger results will be obtained under these conditions than can be hoped for otherwise does not admit of a doubt. That the importance of the Mississippi river, the magnitude of the interests depending upon it, and its influence as a factor in the prosperity of the whole country, deserve and demand the most complete and perfect improvement attainable is equally certain.

If any proposition more than another is inconsistent with everything that has been stated in this paper, it is one which has obtained wide currency and on which opposition to levee building is largely based, that levees cause deposits in the channel and thereby raise the bed of the river. The votaries of this doctrine ignore the testimony of the Mississippi itself, which is conclusive against them, and depend upon an alleged analogy with the Yellow river of China, about which no one knows anything, and with the Po, of which everything that is known refutes their hypothesis.

Another argument against the attempt to confine the floods is that it is an impossible undertaking; that it never has been accomplished and never can be. The facts are that the flood of 1890 was the largest on record from Helena to the Gulf; that it was confined between levees over the same distance with a loss of only one mile in 300, as against one in 22 in 1882, one in 35 in 1883 and one in 120 in 1884. If this be failure what is success? A reasonable man will not abandon a cherished undertaking while his resources are unexhausted, and his last effort is markedly more successful than any previous one.

With the advantages of levees unappreciated, their difficulties exaggerated and dangers asserted when none exist, it is small wonder that the cause has languished, and that its active advocates have been suspected of carrying their convictions and their purses in the same pocket. Private interest has compelled the residents of the Mississippi valley to study the question, and study it deeply. They have learned by that study that there is a public interest, which will be benefited jointly with their private welfare by the construction and maintenance of a system of levees, and their appeal has no more sinister purpose than to secure an equitable cooperation of that joint interest in the pursuit of the common object.

THE MISSISSIPPI RIVER.—HOW TO CONTROL.

[Maj. T. G. DABNEY, Chief Engineer of the Yazoo-Mississippi Delta Levee District.]

The problem of successfully regulating and controlling the Mississippi river is one of great magnitude, financially and otherwise, and of absorbing importance to enormous interests, a vast territory and several millions of people.

Arguments have so often been arrayed to prove that this is a work of national importance, and within the proper province of the national government, that I will not here attempt to discuss that phase of the question; neither will I here undertake to treat it from an economic standpoint, but confine my remarks to its engineering features. The problem is one which I believe does not present any grave engineering difficulties, the obstacles to success consisting mainly of two, namely, magnitude of the cost and hindrance of the engineer's plans by the interference of non-experts.

In considering the first-named obstacle we are necessarily drawn into a discussion of the vital imperfections of the whole system of internal improvements as carried on by the United States government—imperfections which render efforts in this direction to a great extent nugatory. This arises from the incompatibility which subsists between works of practical engineering and political domination in their control and in the source of money supply. This means that a well-established system of procedure is necessary, and a prompt, certain and sufficient supply of means, an absolute essential to any considerable degree of success in great works of this character. Both of the above essentials are lacking in our governmental system of internal improvements, hence we spend large sums of money with but small returns, and the face of the country is sprinkled over with unfinished works in a state of perpetual incompletion. It is safe to say that if the affairs of corporations were generally conducted on similar principles it would not be possible at this day to run a train of cars all the way through from New Orleans to New York.

Captain James B. Eads made a grand success of his work for improving the mouth of the Mississippi river. It is true that under his contract the work cost the government nearly three times as much as the estimate of the United States engineers amounted to, which, by the way, was the cause of their opposition to his scheme, a fact not generally recognized in the popular mind.

The investors in the jetty scheme realized more than 150 per cent. on their investments, but it was money well expended, because a great good was accomplished; whereas, if the government had undertaken to do the work through their own agents, it would in all probability never have been completed under our system of fitful and insufficient appropriations and constant interference by Congress with the plans of the engineers.

The report of the chief of engineers made to the Fiftieth Congress, set forth that after making all the reductions in his estimates that he possibly could, he found that he could not get along without $40,000,000 for the approaching season's work. The rivers and harbors committee calmly cut down all estimates with little or no discrimination, so as to make an aggregate of one-half that sum, under the conviction that Congress would not appropriate a greater amount.

The present rivers and harbors bill hangs in the balance, its fate depending upon political exigencies, while incomplete projects in various parts of the country are going to waste for want of funds to continue them; and officers in charge of suspended works are holding their working organizations together as best they can under great strain, and doing their best to keep their plant and machinery from falling into useless decay until the fate of this bill shall be determined. In the meantime a favorable working season is rapidly passing away, and Congress is oblivious to these matters. But this question has been ably treated by Senator Cullom and other statesmen, and will not be further elaborated here.

In 1879 the United States, recognizing the national importance of regulating the lower Mississippi river in the interest of navigation, by an act of Congress caused the appointment of a commission of experts to take the matter in charge, which was undoubtedly the proper course to pursue. This nation is probably not inferior to any other in the engineering ability available for such a purpose. The government has at their command a highly skillful and experienced corps of military engineers, and the civil branch of the profession in this country cannot be surpassed in any other for skill and professional enterprise.

Both branches of the profession, as well as the coast survey organization, were called upon to make up the personnel of the Mississippi River Commission. It is then a body of scientific experts who are presumably eminently qualified to deal with the problem which was placed in their hands.

The magnitude of the problem presented and the uniqueness of its important features necessitated much careful preliminary research and study before deciding upon definite plans of procedure, and while the principles to be applied might be fixed and certain to begin with, yet the practical methods used were necessarily tentative, requiring to be modified as the work developed.

But the Congress and the public demanded results after the first season's operations before it was possible for definite results to be realized, and very soon legislators essayed to play the role of engineers, questioning the soundness of the river commission's plans and demanding changes. Appropriations were at times withheld altogether, and when given were insufficient in amount and coupled with restrictive conditions which greatly embarrassed the engineers in their efforts to prosecute the work. In this connection, it is especially noticeable that Congressmen made war, and Congress placed restrictions, upon the most essential and valuable feature in the plans of the river commission for the regulation and control of the great river, to wit: the application of bank revetment to prevent caving; for the one factor—caving banks—is the one great obstacle to the solution of the problem, and the work of giving stability to the banks and consequent fixedness to the position of the channel, is the key to that solution.

The plan of the commission at the beginning of their work embodied three principal features, which were regarded as holding a relative importance as in the order named, to wit: first, the contraction of the low-water channel in shoal places; second, the protection of caving banks, and third, the building up of artificial banks (levees) to prevent overflow of flood water. Of these, Congress showed a desire to eliminate or greatly restrict, the last two, and confine the work to the first.

After ten years of experiments, the river commission would now prefer to limit the first to a minimum, and expend most of their efforts on the other two.

It is my own conviction that further development will show the bank protection to be the *sine qua non* to ultimate and complete success. The restraining of the floods is next in importance, while the deepening of the bar crossings by low-water channel contraction will be considered useful only as a temporary device to give present relief while the more durable work is in progress.

Perfect stability of the banks of the Mississippi river would in time correct all the other irregularities, and would prove sufficient in itself to both create a deep channel throughout the river's entire length, except at its mouth, and prevent the overflow of its flood waters.

This work, however, by reason of its extensiveness and cost, would consume time in its accomplishment, and adding the factor of uncertain appropriations and the time becomes indefinite.

Furthermore, the process of assuming a new and permanent regimen would be gradual, and during the period of transformation levees would be necessary to restrain the floods and prevent a further aggravation of existing evils. There can be no doubt that levees alone, if properly maintained, would ameliorate, if not entirely remove, the obstructions to navigation, by the tendency exerted to lower the crests of the bars on crossings at the reversionary points between bends, whereas the dispersion of the flood water, when unrestrained by levees, will have the opposite effect of elevating them. It is also a patent fact that levees are essential to the ease and safety of high-water navigation, a fact which has not been sufficiently emphasized heretofore.

The application of the principle of low-water channel contraction will also be found useful and necessary to hasten the removal of the more serious obstacles to navigation at low-water stages. But if the banks of the river are allowed to continue the caving process, the artificially deepened channels would soon be deserted by the withdrawal of the volume of water intended to occupy them, and they be incorporated within the shore line opposite the receding bank.

The maintenance of efficient levees with facility is

also dependent upon giving stability to the banks, as the great burden of cost in their maintenance is due to the necessity of constantly renewing those portions that cave into the river, and each successive renewal must be made on lower ground, and consequently at greater cost.

In allusions to the scouring action of the current to deepen the channel, there is much apprehension. The channel itself is abundantly deep everywhere, and needs no further scouring; but it is obstructed every few miles by immense deposits of sand and mud, which have a general tendency to shift along down stream. Between these obstructions the water is very deep, from 50 to 100 feet at low water. But the effective depth for navigation and the capacity for voiding flood water must be measured by the height above the sand hills, and the intervening deep water counts for nothing. When the river is at flood height the current has immense erosive power from the great impetus with which it strikes the concave banks in the bends. This produces violent caving, and enormous quantities of silt are taken up by the water and carried to the next shoal below, where it is deposited, or a great part of it. The same operation goes on in each successive bend of the river, which usually follow one another in quick succession. By this operation the shoal places rise as the river rises, keeping even pace with it. Then, when the flood subsides and the surface is lowered, the caving diminishes, and ceases altogether when low water is reached. The water being thus deprived of the material afforded by the caving banks reaches the shoal, not only without a load to drop, but with power to pick up some of that recently deposited and carry it over into the bend below, thus lowering the crusts of the bars as the river declines.

During flood periods these bars attain an elevation much above that of the low-water surface, so that if the river were reduced suddenly from high to low water, the channel would have hundreds of dams across it, and the water would cease to flow entirely until it rose high enough to overtop each dam successively.

It can be readily understood, therefore, that with a completed system of bank protection, by which caving would cease altogether, the water would not be charged with material wherewith to build up the bars as it rose to flood height, but, on the contrary, would charge over them with a greatly increased scouring capacity which would speedily carry their crusts forward into the deep water beyond, resulting in the creation of a uniformity of depth, which would not only insure good navigation at all stages, but so increase the voiding capacity of the channel as to greatly lower the flood level and bring it within the natural banks, except, perhaps, where they are abnormally low, where some levee construction would be necessary. From Baton Rouge to the Gulf the caving is very slight, and, as a consequence, there are no shoals in that part of the river.

The floods are not there confined within the natural banks of the river, because the slope is too flat to admit of rapid voidance of the water into the Gulf.

In considering the cost of a complete application of this principle for the regulation of the Mississippi river, which I venture to predict will ultimately be done, it may be assumed that no bank revetment will be needed below Baton Rouge. The distance from Cairo to that point is 830 miles; add 370 miles for the Yazoo front, and we have 1,200 miles of bank to treat. But it is probably safe to say that only about one-third of this entire length will require the application of revetment work to actually caving banks. The maximum cost of that kind of work as at present developed is $18 per lineal foot of bank, or say, $95,000 per mile. Then we have as the total cost $95,000 by 400 miles equal $38,000,000. This, with $10,000,000 for levees and, say, $6,000,000 for channel contraction, making $54,-000,000, will represent about the total cost to the government of completely regulating and controlling the most valuable navigable stream in the world.

It may be assumed that the three principal features in the work of the commission, as embodied in the first plan announced by them, are still necessary to be adhered to, but their relative value and importance in the scheme must be changed, so that bank protection shall rank first, levees second and channel contraction third, though in the order of prosecution all should proceed co-ordinately, the last two being quite essential for immediate effects.

A doubt has been cast upon the efficacy of levees to restrain the floods of the Mississippi river, owing to a greater or less extent of breakage in every very high water that has occurred. This skepticism on the part of some is perhaps natural, but is based upon a very puerile sort of reasoning, the usual formula being "the levees can't be made to stand because they never have been made to stand." It is patent, however, that the levees have broken in some places because they were too weak in those places; had they been strong enough they would have held, as they did under the same pressure generally throughout extensive unbroken lines. In this connection it may be mentioned that during the extraordinary flood of the past spring there was on the Yazoo front 180 miles of levee, extending southward from the head of this basin with but one small break, having only a local effect, and that this line of levee protected from overflow about 5,000 square miles of territory, or about 80 per cent. of the Yazoo basin.

In considering the question of levee efficiency in the light of experience, it is necessary to bear in mind the history of levee development up to the present time. Without going too largely into detail it may be stated that levees have never been constructed on scientific principles, but, in fact, in the crudest possible manner. This has not been due to any shortcoming on the part of levee engineers or levee projectors, but simply to the want of means to do better. Thus engineers have been compelled to adopt minimum dimensions for levees and to pile up simple dirt in the cheapest possible way with little or no regard to the best methods of construction, almost entirely ignoring the preparation of the foundation, burying stumps, roots and sunken logs without any effort to remove them, this work being precluded by the extra cost of doing it, so that in 15 or 20 years these levees become leaky and unsafe and occasionally collapse under pressure, because of cavities under them resulting from the decay of the perishable matter so incorporated in the structures. In many cases levees have been located too near to caving banks with a consciousness that they could last only a few years, because to select a safer location would involve a longer and more costly line when money was not available for its construction. From this necessity levee administration has been the reverse of economical in all respects, and at the same time insufficient to a great degree.

All of these considerations have conjoined to create a low esteem for the levees in the minds of the people, so that with the lapse of a few successive low water years they have been subjected to great abuse in cutting them down with wagons and general traffic, and laws enacted for their preservation have been ignored. The result has been that an occasional extraordinary flood has come and found the levees in a dilapidated condition, mainly from neglect and abuse, with numerous weak places, some of which have always yielded to the pressure of the water.

Now all of this is easily susceptible of correction, the principal factor being a sufficiency of money to construct new levees, where needed, upon simple common sense principles, by making safe foundations, removing all perishable matter from beneath them and paying proper regard to the best method of construction, as, for example, rigidly excluding all "station work," which is work sublet by the "station" to individual laborers, and requiring all that can be so treated to be done with teams and scrapers. This alone would be an important and valuable revolution in the prevailing methods of levee building.

Existing old levees, where they have shown weakness, should be strengthened hy enlargement where necessary, but especially should their foundations be improved by deep and capacious excavations under the base, by which defects would be disclosed and removed, and the excavation refilled with sound and well-compacted material.

The next requisite is to enact proper laws for the preservation of the levees, and require their rigid enforcement.

The question of proper grade lines for levees has been a very complex problem, owing to the great diversity of the conditions under which different floods have come. This has been largely due to an incomplete levee system, by which large volumes of water have escaped from the river in some localities and returned to it in others, and to caving banks, which have resulted in "cut-offs" that gave rise to great aberrations in the flood plane. The question of grade lines has, therefore, been largely guess work in the absence of certain and regular data upon which to fix them. But deficiency in elevation is not near so important as imperfect foundation and base. With a good and sound levee underneath, having sufficient base and crown, it is not at all difficult to keep out a flood that overtops the levee by two feet or more.

All of this points to the fact that a more thorough system of levee building is needed, and that a much larger sum of money should be available at one time than all the local levee organizations combined are able to command.

Since the United States government has logically and confessedly an interest in restraining the floods of the Mississippi river at least equal to that of the riparian States, and since the latter have already expended sums greatly in excess of the whole government expenditure in this work, there is little room for argument on the question that the United States ought now to take prompt and effective measures, in co-operation with the States, to create, without further delay, a complete and perfect system of levees throughout the entire delta of the Mississippi river.

This is a part of the work of river improvement that can be accomplished with certainty and promptitude, and when done definite and exceedingly valuable results will be at once attained.

I would suggest, as a practical measure which would seem to meet the equities of the case and reconcile difficulties which exist in the minds of some persons, that there be a distinct recognition of a community of interests in the levees, as between the riparian States on the one side and the general government on the other side, and that each party assume a definite *pro rata* share of the cost of building and maintaining them according to a basis of division to be agreed upon. Then let each party come forward with its contribution in sufficient amount to ensure the completion of a general levee system with as little delay as practicable.

Whenever the government makes up their minds to proceed in earnest to permanently regulate and improve the Mississippi river, the way to do so can be pointed out in very simple fashion. Let Congress place at the disposal of the Mississippi River Commission such sums of money as they shall make requisition for from year to year upon estimates submitted by them, and allow them to go on with the work without further interference or restrictions on the part of Congress. This is how similar works are accomplished by other governments, and it is the only way in which it can be done.

THE MISSISSIPPI RIVER—ITS PHENOMENA AND PHYSICAL TREATMENT.

[MAJOR WM. STARLING, Chief Engineer.]

Every man who is in the habit of making journeys on the great lines of railway has probably observed some of the phenomena of alluvial valleys, for these are selected by the engineers as a bed already partially graded by nature for their roadways. In ascending a mountain range, instead of excavating, escarping and tunneling a road for ourselves, we have only to find in the lowlands a river, the general direction of whose course corresponds, as nearly as may be to the route sought by us, and then following the stream upward toward one of its sources. In this manner we are conducted by an ascent, easy and gentle at first, afterwards steeper and steeper, to the dividing ridge, whence, by a reversal of the former process, we gradually descend to the plains on the other side. Those whose faculties are not buried in sleep or benumbed by a dull novel will have observed that the river, after running between iron-bound rocks, expands occasionally into broad and fertile "bottoms," becoming wider, longer and more continuous as we descend. These bottoms are bounded on either side by the highlands which have served to limit the excursions of the river, and this latter wanders through the valley, skirting the base of the hills, now on this side, now on that, pursuing a tortuous course through the bed which it has made for itself; for the bottoms are the work of the river—are composed of sediment brought down in time of flood, and spread far and wide as the swollen stream overflowed its narrow banks. Being the product of the stream, they are composed of pulverized material, free, for the most part, of stones and heavy fragments. Being formed by overflow, they can never rise above the level of the stream in flood; indeed, can never attain the height of extreme floods, and must always be liable to overflow in great freshets.

Thus the valley, continuous it may be in itself, is divided into a series of subordinate basins, each bounded by the river on the one hand and the hills on the other, and terminated, above and below, by the close approach of the highlands to the stream.

What occurs to creeks and mountain streams on the small scale, occurs also to the greatest rivers. The history of the Ohio and Mississippi is a good deal the same as the history of the rivulets from which they originate, multiplied a thousand-fold. The most insignificant meadow-brook is a Mississippi in miniature; and the student of river engineering has often spent most profitable hours in contemplating, on a scale which may be easily embraced by the eye and the understanding, phenomena which embarass and bewilder him when presented with magnificence and complexity which attend the operations of a mighty river.

In mountainous countries creek-bottoms are of great importance on account of their unexampled fertility, all the more, as distinguished from the stony and arid tracts which surround them. Offering no impediments to the plough, being nearly level, and having excellent drainage, they possess unusual advantages for cultivation. They have but one drawback. A flood of unusual height may submerge them, and the farmer may loose his labor partially or wholly—partially, if the flood be not very great, or occur so early that the crop may be replanted; wholly, under very unfavorable circumstances, for not only may the overflow occur late in the season, when the greatest outlay has been incurred, and the owner is about to reap his return, but the flood may be of such magnitude as to sweep away the accumulated labor of former years—fences, stables, even dwellings, and may go so far as to cause loss of life itself.

Overflows occur, of course, because the ordinary channel of the stream is not sufficient to contain the unusual quantity of water poured forth at the height of the flood; neither can it ever become sufficient under the operation of purely natural causes. The stream has built for itself a bed, distributing its sedimentary matter beyond its banks, and preserving for itself a channel suited to its ordinary wants. Great floods occur too seldom, and endure too short a time to exercise a marked influence in enlarging the channel by their excavating power.

So valuable are the bottom lands that they are almost always cultivated in spite of the danger of overflow. It is natural, however, that means should be sought to protect them from this calamity. Now, to give flood plains immunity from inundation, only one means exists; that is, to make the river-channel large enough to hold all the water, ordinary or extraordinary, that can possibly be poured into it. To enlarge the channel we must adopt one of two alternatives—dig its bottom deeper or wider, or build its banks higher. The latter being by far the easier and cheaper process is the expedient commonly adopted; the more, that it does not exclude the former, nor is at all antagonistic to it, but, on the contrary, facilitates it and co-operates with it.

Thus, the system of artificial embankments or *levees*, as the French settlers called them, naturally suggests itself wherever there are alluvial bottoms or flood plains of considerable extent. It is a method which cannot generally be used with advantage on a small scale for several reasons. When streams are ordinarily inconsiderable, with high freshets and the flood plains narrow, levees are expensive and out of proportion to the benefit to be derived. In narrow valleys the line would have to be very long to protect an insignificant area. Not only so, but being hemmed in between the hills on one side and the levees on the other, there would be no drainage, and the injury from rain and surface water would perhaps be greater than from overflow.

The method of protection by means of levees is then peculiarly applicable in the case of large rivers with very wide valleys, and under these circumstances it has long been successfully practiced. The question of drainage, however, is still a serious one. The great basins are usually heavily overgrown with timber. Evaporation is consequently very slow, and the accumulation of rain and surface water is very great, especially in the lower part of the protected area. For it must be remembered that bottom lands are by no means level in the strict sense of the word, but follow the fall of the flood line—that is, they slope toward the sea. Therefore, if drainage be free, all the water which collects in an enclosed area will accumulate at the lower end. This aggregation will not only occupy a great space which might profitably be reclaimed, but will greatly impede the free flow of drainage waters from the upper part of the area. Consequently, in a strictly enclosed basin, it is found necessary to provide pumps or equivalent means of getting rid of the surplus waters. Culverts may be used, but, of course, are available only after the flood waters have begun to recede.

In the case of a very large basin it may be found the best plan to leave the tower part thereof entirely open. This portion will thus be subject to overflow, but only to a limited extent. For the flood waters, entering at the very foot of the basin—that is, at the lowest possible elevation—cannot mount higher than the level of that part of the stream. As the flood plain has a considerable slope, the upper part will be perfectly dry. For instance, the fall of the flood plain of the Mississippi river from Memphis to Vicksburg is about two-thirds of a foot to the mile. The average height of the greatest floods above the surface of this flood plain is perhaps eight feet. Suppose a system of levees, complete in its upper part, to terminate abruptly at any given point. Then at that point the land will be overflowed eight feet. Twelve miles above the land will be just a wash. Twenty-four miles above the land will be eight feet out of water.

The course which has been prescribed for theoretical reasons has been made compulsory in the case of the Mississippi by the intervention of tributaries. Every basin of considerable size must of necessity have an auxiliary stream or streams to drain it into the main river. Usually, from the nature of the case, the drainage is concentrated into one stream. The borders of the main river are high, for they receive the bulk of the deposit, as fresh quantities of loaded water are continually arriving, which drop the greater portion of their burden, as soon as they become dispersed, and afterwards less and less as the water becomes more stagnant and clearer. Thus, small streams, tributary to the main river, or inlet bayous as they are called, are rare. The course of drainage almost always is from the high alluvial ridge on the bank of the river to the low lands in the interior, and eventually to the main tributary which skirts the hills, and at the foot of its basin discharges into the Mississippi. These tributaries are usually of such magnitude that it would be well-nigh impossible to levee them. They receive, beside the drainage of the alluvial basin proper, large accessions from minor streams which descend from the hills, so that even if they could be leveed the volume of water thus imprisoned behind the levee would be portentiously great, too great to be pumped out or discharged in any reasonable time through a culvert, so their mouths have to be left open perforce. The basins narrow toward the lower end, so that the quantity of land damaged is still further reduced.

The valley of the Mississippi, like all others, is divided into a number of subordinate basins by the approach of the hills on either side. Some of these basins are very small, others are of enormous extent. Each is in a great measure independent of the others, so that the task of protection from overflow is much simplified and rendered more practicable, as it does not necessarily require a vast and simultaneous organized effort, or even a continuous system, but may be effected in detail, according to the needs and abilities of separate sections.

The small basins do not afford the best field for the application of the levee system for reasons already given, and for the additional reason that in them backwater from the mouth of the tributary is destructive out of proportion. For instance, if the influence of backwater is more or less detrimental 15 miles above the mouth of the tributary, and the basin be only 20 miles long, then three-fourths of it will be more or less liable to injury in time of flood. But if the basin be 150 miles long, then only one-tenth will suffer.

It is to the great basins, consequently, that we must look for examples of successful protection by levees. Below Cairo the Mississippi has four such basins, drained respectively by the Saint Francis, the Yazoo, the Tensas and the Atchafalaya rivers and their tributaries. The last three have been wholly or partially leveed for many years. The nearest approximation to a complete system has been made on the Yazoo front.

The Yazoo basin has every advantage that the engineer could ask for a fair trial of the levee system. It begins a short distance below Memphis and extends to a point a little above Vicksburg. At each of these localities the highlands actually abut upon the Mississippi river, thus completely isolating the basin, and affording a secure support for the ends of the line of levees. The front of the basin, measured according to the sinuosities of the Mississippi, is about three hundred and fifty miles long. In a straight line the distance is about one hundred and eighty miles. Its shape is lenticular, the Yazoo hills forming one arc and the Mississippi river the other. Its extreme breadth is about sixty miles. There are no "inlet bayous," the drainage being altogether toward the interior, and eventually into the Yazoo river. This, under one name or another, skirts the base of the hills, and empties into the main river just above Vicksburg.

The entire front of the Yazoo basin is closed by a continuous embankment, extending from the uplands below Memphis to within about eight miles of the mouth of the Yazoo. This embankment does not strictly follow the line of the river, but sometimes takes short cuts, so that its length is about three hundred miles. The material of which it is composed is earth entirely.

It is usually eight feet wide on top. The height is defined by reference to some great flood, usually the most recent. The prevailing grade before the flood of the present year was from three to five feet, according to circumstances, above the high water of 1882. The angle of inclination of each of the slopes of the embankment, front and back, is fixed by the proportion three of base to one of altitude, though sometimes the dimensions fall short of these and sometimes they exceed them. In fact, both in height and strength, the levees are somewhat irregular.

The causes of these variations in construction are not usually to be sought in any scientific considerations. They are due, for the most part, to the haphazard manner in which the levees were built. Originally constructed by private enterprise for the reclamation of partial areas, they have been connected, raised, enlarged, repaired, demolished by crevasse and overflow, wiped out of existence by caving into the river and replaced by entirely new lines joined to the old at suitable places, as necessity dictated or financial conditions permitted. The system is a patchwork, in fact, the result of many different periods, organizations and administrations, having diverse views of policy and managed with all possible differences of ability and resources. To enter into a minute history of the levee system would probably be neither interesting nor profitable, except to a professed student of that subject. With reference to the Yazoo front, it may be sufficient to say that the close of the civil war found in existence two "levee districts," as they are called, each containing several counties, and embracing together the whole Yazoo basin. Of these, the upper, or District No. 1, fell into bad hands, in the confusion and misgovernment of the reconstrction period, and eventually lapsed into complete decay, and its levees were suffered to go to ruin. The lower district was then reorganized and rebaptized as the Mississippi levee district, and has maintained a flourishing existence, under one name or the other, for the last twenty-five years. In 1884 the counties not included in this district were incorporated into a new organization called the Yazoo-Mississippi delta levee district, which thus consists substantially of nearly the same territory as old district No. 1, but is to be carefully distinguished from it, as it does not and should not inherit the evil reputation or the unpaid obligation of that corporation.

As at present organized, the levees of the Yazoo front are maintained by two districts, each with its own organization and its own methods of raising revenues. The supreme governing bodies of these districts are called levee boards. They consist of one or more members from each county in the district. They are armed with a good deal of authority, with power to impose taxes up to a certain limit, to condemn lands, and to exercise all functions incidental to the building and maintenance of levees. They elect their own officers and fix their own rates of salaries.

The territory embraced within these districts are mutually dependent on the levees of the other. The lower district would be partially overflowed by breaks in the

MISSISSIPPI RIVER IMPROVEMENT. 89

upper; and certain counties of the upper district lie behind those of the lower, and would be affected by any breaks in the levees of the latter. Attempts have been made to consolidate the whole administration in the hands of one board, but serious obstacles have been found to exist in the different rates and manners of taxation of the two districts, their debts and a diversity of local interests. So far, very little practical inconvenience has been found in the division of territory, the two organizations having worked together very harmoniously.

It might seem a very simple matter to build earthworks sufficient to turn water, but in reality it is a very complex problem. With unlimited means, of course mountains could be thrown up, by the rudest of engineering, that would keep out the greatest of possible floods. But it is never the case that means are unlimited. Be they never so great, it is the engineer's business to extend them economically, to accomplish his objects without waste or extravagance. But the means in this case are not only limited, but scanty. Therefore, the least possible margin can be allowed for contingencies, and minute economies must be studied.

Levees, to fulfill their purpose, must be high enough and strong enough, must rest on a secure foundation and must not be subject to deterioration beyond a known and remediable extent.

The strength of an earthen embankment depends on its shape, its thickness and the quality of the material which composes it. The stronger and heavier the earth, the less the thickness required. Now, with a due regard to economy, it is hardly possible to use any other material than that which is found on the spot. This may be clay, sand, loam, or all together, arranged in their strata. Nothing is more common than to find a thickness of one or two feet of the stiff, black clay of the Mississippi valley, commonly called "buck-shot" earth, overlying a stratum of nearly pure sand. Very frequently the reverse is the case, the lighter soil lying on the surface and the heavier beneath. Thus it may, and generally does, happen that the levee is not even homogeneous in each of its several parts, but is composed of widely different materials in all manner of varying proportions.

The pressure of water increases uniformly with the depth at the rate of about $62\frac{1}{2}$ pounds per foot. It is nothing at all at the surface. Therefore, were the water always to remain absolutely still, could the greatest height to which it could ever come be accurately predicted, and could the embankment be depended upon to remain perfectly unchanged, the cross-section of the levee would be a simple triangle with merely enough base to give a weight that should keep from either overturning or sliding, which would be a matter of easy calculation, and of a height barely equal to that of the greatest floods.

But not one of these conditions holds good. The water is lashed by storms and temporarily raised by winds, sometimes to a considerable extent. It has never yet been satisfactorily demonstrated what would be the maximum height attained by the water during a flood equal to that of say 1882. Unfortunately, in this and all other great floods, the levees have given way at numerous places before the culmination of the wave, and it is a matter of inference how much higher the water would have gone if perfectly confined. Previously to the present year the levees were in too imperfect a state and observations too scanty to authorize any positive conclusions. Very diverse opinions were entertained on the subject by eminent engineers, according as each laid the principal stress on one or another element of the problem. This year it is thought that a close approximation has been made, and that it is known, within a small fraction of a foot, how great an elevation would have been reached by the flood had all the levees held.

But floods are not all alike. Some come mainly from the Ohio, some come from the Missouri, some derive great accessions from the lower tributaries. Some come with great rapidity, as a single tremendous wave; some consist of a series of minor fluctuations, terminated perhaps by the greatest of all. Some come in February or March, some in June or July. These circumstances all exert a great influence on the relative height of the water at different parts of the river. Thus the flood of 1883 (a sharp one from the Ohio) attained a stage of more than 52 feet on the gauge at Cairo, and less than 44 feet at Vicksburg. The flood of 1890 (a succession of slow rises, terminating in two great waves) reached less than 49 feet at Cairo and more than 49 feet at Vicksburg.

It is impracticable, then, to fix with precision the greatest height at any point possibly to be attained by the water. There must, therefore, be a margin of safety allowed in prescribing the height to be given to a levee, not only on this account, but from a regard to the possible and highly probable prevalence of high winds and waves during flood. So, also, one cross-section can no longer be a triangle, running to an edge at the top. The crown must be broadened for greater strength and for the sake of a foothold for the workmen while putting up revetments or other temporary defenses against storms, as well as to serve as a base for a "topping" or raising of the levee in an emergency.

Again, earth will not maintain either its height or its shape unaltered, especially if exposed to the wash, percolation or pressure, or all combined, of water. Earth, when thrown into an embankment, suffers shrinkage, as it is technically called, which differs exceedingly according to the quality of the earth used and the method of construction, being greatest for dry clay thrown up with wheelbarrows and least for sand put in with scrapers. Engineers attempt to make allowance for this shrinkage, but at best they can make only rough estimates founded on an examination of the soil, and from a consideration of the mode of construction, the weather and all the circumstances, and there is always the possibility of error. Therefore, a levee will sometimes settle below its proper height without any extraordinary cause, and before the water has ever been against it. Rains assist in this deterioration by washing the slopes before they are firmly sodded.

But no matter how well an embankment be constructed, if it be built of earth alone, when water stands long against it it is subject to percolation, which softens and disintegrates the material. Earths, when thrown up and allowed to take their natural slopes, assume very different angles according as they are dry or wet, and different earths show a wide diversity of behavior in this regard. The general tendency is the same, however. The wet slope is uniformly flatter than the dry. The floods of the Mississippi always last weeks and sometimes months, thus giving the water abundant time to penetrate the interior of the embankments. This it frequently does effectually, so that the whole levee is sometimes saturated.

Now, wet earth is as good to keep out water as dry, provided it can be made to maintain its form. That it may be certain to do this in the case proposed, the slope given to the earth must not be less than the normal "wet slope" of that earth, otherwise the bank will of itself tend to assume that slope, and widen the base at the expense of its height. Usually the first manifestation of such a tendency is the "sloughing" of the back slope, by which great masses of earth slide from the embankment and form a pasty quagmire at the foot of the slope. It is evident that a continuation of this process means eventual disruption. Fortunately the movement is not usually difficult to check if plenty of men and material are at hand. This, however, is not always the case. Earth is frequently very scarce in time of high water. Moreover, emergency work is very expensive and precarious; therefore it is best to build embankments at once to the required strength.

As has been previously stated, however, there is a great diversity in the soils composing the alluvium of the Mississippi valley, and three or four qualities are likely to be encountered in the construction of a single work—nay, even to be intermingled in the same bank. It is often very difficult to decide which is the prevailing quality, much more to decide in advance, for the guidance of assistant engineers and contractors. In this uncertainty it has very commonly been the practice to build levees by a rough rule, supposed to be safe in the average of soils, of making the base of each slope, front and back, three times the height. The total base of the levee will thus be six times the height, *plus* the width of the crown, usually eight or ten feet. Levees of these dimensions will generally stand, with water to the very top, even in soils weaker than the average. Neither is it a great waste to give the same proportions to embankments built of stronger material, to wit, of "buckshot" clay, if put up loosely with wheelbarrows and exposed to the pressure of the water while yet "green," for such banks are very porous and apt to leak and slough if of inadequate dimensions. Still another reason for a broad base will be given in the sequel. In the absence, then, of definite reasons to the contrary, levees have usually been built with slopes of three to one.

Where there is great exposure to the action of winds and waves these dimensions are modified, the outer or front slope being made flatter and the inner slope steepened or not, according to circumstances. It has not usually been found good policy to make the back or land slope very steep, for fear of sloughing. After completion the whole work is sodded with Bermuda grass, which puts out lateral runners, taking root at the joints, and thus spreads rapidly, covering the slopes, in a year's time, with a thick mat of sod.

When a water works engineer is called upon to build an embankment for a reservoir, the first thing he looks to is his foundation. Though his dam be never so massive and tight, it avails him nothing unless it rests upon a secure bed. The levee engineer has seldom been able to take the same precautions. In the first place, they are not so obligatory. The water does not usually stand very high against his embankments, nor does it remain there the year round. He has an ample base. Experience had not formerly been understood as indicating the necessity of devoting special attention to foundations. In short, a good bank placed on the natural soil has been thought sufficient. Usually, indeed, the means have not been forthcoming for any refinements of engineering. The urgent demand has been for earth, and more earth, piled higher and higher and yet higher as the system neared completion. The experience of 1882 seemed to teach that the principal danger to be apprehended was that of the actual overtopping of the levees, and of course the principal efforts have been made with a view of avoiding this imminent peril. With the advances in levee building, however, the more perfect confinement of floods and the new constructions on lower ground, caused by the caving of banks, the levees have had to stand a great deal more water than formerly, and defects in foundations have developed themselves, especially during the past spring, with unmistakable clearness, indicating the necessity for special attention to this detail.

That an earthen bank should be preserved from deterioration, the first and almost the only requisite is that it shall be made of earth only—that is, that no stumps, roots or other perishable matter should be left in it, or immediately under it, which by its decay should leave cavities or conduits. That it may preserve its "grade"—that is, its proper height relative to high water—occasional repairs will be necessary, especially in situations where it is apt to settle, as in crossing the beds of old water-courses, or the like.

A line of levees is, of course, not level from Memphis to Vicksburg, but follows the fall of the river. Now, this fall, or slope, is about a third of a foot to the mile, if taken in the average. Yet he would be a very foolish engineer who should take it for granted that the rate of fall was uniform and should build his levees on that supposition. The river, in fact, is divided into pools and rapids. In the pools the water surface remains nearly level, sometimes for miles, and in the rapids the fall is often as much as three or four times the average.

The reader has now some notion of what a levee should be. Levees as they actually exist do not, however, approximate closely to this ideal for reasons already mentioned. It is the constant effort of those in charge of the different districts to bring them, step by step, nearer to perfection, but they are still far from the goal, though well within sight of it. Knowing their systems to be imperfect, it is with anxious hearts that they face great floods, for the chance of disaster is present every day as a possibility or probability as long as the water is near its height, and the period of trial is sometimes lengthened into months.

The cause of breaks in levees, or crevasses, as they are generally called, after the manner of the Louisiana creoles, are manifold. A failure to comply with any of the necessary conditions of safe levees, as previously defined, may result in a break. Most common of all is mere insufficiency of height. If water is allowed to run over a levee for any length of time it cuts gullies, which widen with tremendous rapidity, especially in sandy soil—this morning it is a thin stream, in an hour it is a cascade; this evening it may be a gap twenty feet wide, to-morrow it may be a thousand. Hence the "overtopping" of the levees by the flood is to be obviated by all possible means, and extraordinary exertions are frequently made with this end. If it be evident that a levee is too low, it must be raised by any means that are at hand. A very common way is by placing plank on edge, two or three courses, if necessary, nailed to short posts, and backing them with earth. This expedient is also well known to the Dutch, who call it *opkisting*, or boxing up, and use it in emergencies, which in their case are usually ice gorges. Loose earth does very well when it can be had in abundance, provided there is no exposure to winds, and provided the crown is wide enough to bear the additional quantity. Sacks sometimes are made to answer an excellent purpose, and can be made into a water-tight wall when well piled and laid carefully in tiers. Many a mile of levee has been triumphantly held in these ways when the water was two feet or more above the top of the old embankment.

As the usual time of spring floods is the beginning of March, the blustering northerly winds of that month playing on the broad expanse of water, brimming full up to the very tops of the levees, create formidable breakers, which, impinging on the front slope of the levees, where the latter are near to the bank of the river and are unprotected by a thick growth of timber, soon cut through the sod of Bermuda grass, thick and strong as it is, and unless met by prompt measures speedily produce a break in the levee. This is the more to be dreaded that both the winds and the waters at that season are freezing cold, and men get benumbed and worn out in contending against them; moreover, the storms last a long time—perhaps 24 or 48 hours, with little intermission, necessitating constant work, night and day. Most dangerous of all is it when a tempest of wind and rain spring up at night and unwilling men have to be roused from sleep and from comfortable quarters to face a howling norther, with rain and sleet accompaniment and breakers dashing clean over the levee. In such emergencies the sovereign remedy is sacks, well filled, sewed with strong twine, placed in position in lieu of the earth cut away by the waves, and serving as a protection to the portion of the levee which is still intact. I have yet to see a storm so violent that it cannot be successfully resisted with plenty of good men and of large, new, strong sacks, and with a broad enough crown to furnish material and good footing, for there is no time to make long excursions for earth; it must usually be taken from the levee itself—as far as possible from the front slope, which would otherwise be simply wasted by the cutting of the waves; then from the back as sparingly as may be. If there be time for preparation, of course sacks are filled from a distance and placed on top of the levee ready for use. Lumber also is provided and made into revetments to protect the front slope, being well backed up either with filled sacks or with strong earth. In short, the devices for "high-water fighting," as it is generally and appropriately called, are as numerous as the different turns of ingenuity of the devisers. A good high-water man will turn anything to account—rails, cotton stalks, bagging or what not, and will generally hold his levee, no matter how exposed, if it is high enough, or if it is not high enough, provided it be not exposed.

A third cause of breaks in levees, and one much dreaded by engineers, is unsoundness. An unsound levee is one which, through fraud, negligence or ignorance in the constructors, is filled with decaying stumps or logs. Most such levees are inherited from a former time, when less attention was paid to details and supervision was less strict. Some of them are founded on old private levees, thrown up at short notice in the readiest and cheapest way, and subsequently enlarged and made public. Ugly and dangerous cavities are frequently developed in such banks, and sometimes destruction has been escaped by a hair's breadth. There are stories of holes in levees so big that sacks filled with earth passed through them whole, and wheelbarrows were the only obstructions that could be made to lodge in them. On one occasion a feather-bed passed through whole. Much more common are the small cavities or conduits, usually called "crayfish holes," from the fact that these crustacea inhabit them. For this reason the crayfish are generally considered the authors of the evil, their habit of boring holes being well known. There is a superstition among the Irish laborers, who make a practice of working on levees, against killing a crayfish. They cannot be made to do it, either by threats or by ridicule. They say he is "the poor man's friend;" that is, he provides occupation for the laborer by causing breaks in levees and consequent repairs and rebuilding. Notwithstanding the wide prevalence of this opinion, I think very few levee engineers coincide in it. Their idea is that the cavities mostly proceed from decaying vegetable matter. When a levee is built through timbered land, the practice has usually been to cut down the trees as close to the ground as possible. This regulation has not always been strictly enforced, and frequently a considerable portion of the stump is left. Equally important are the large lateral roots that penetrate the ground horizontally in all directions. With the lapse of years, both stumps and roots decay and leave cavities both in and under the embankment, forming channels through which the water is forced under pressure, making a spouting-hole on the land side. According to this view, the crayfish is merely a tenant, though he may perhaps contribute his labor in enlarging, developing and connecting the cavities. I have had hundreds, perhaps thousands, of these holes cut out, and in almost or quite all cases a decaying stump or root was found to be the radical cause.

Sipe-holes,* as they may be called, sometimes reveal their point of entrance under the water by a suck or vortex. When they can be discovered they are easily stopped from the outside. When they cannot be thus located, the best and most common remedy is to "hoop" them—that is, throw a small semi-circular levee around them, connected with the main levee at each end. This hoop is not built to the level of the outside water, but, perhaps, three or four feet below it. The water that "sipes" through the hole thus rises and overflows the hoop, and is conducted away by a spout. The pressure of the external water is partially borne by the main levee and partly transferred to the hoop. Meanwhile, the current of water through the sipe-hole is so deadened that it is rendered incapable of scouring

---

*All leakage or transpiration through or under a levee, or through the natural ground, usually goes by the general term of sipage or sipe-water (pronounced seep), from the Dutch *sijpelen*, which means the same thing.

out or enlarging the hole, and thus increasing the danger. This treatment is nearly always successful, but requires some little time.

"Sloughing" of the back or land slope of levees is sometimes, though not frequently, the cause of a crevasse. This has already been mentioned as a consequence of too great steepness on that side. It also frequently occurs where levees have recently been enlarged on the land side, and indicates a want of union between the old and the new earth. Sometimes it is due to sipeholes within the base of the levee. From whatever cause it may proceed, it is a formidable danger and requires immediate attention. To the novice nothing is more alarming than an extensive slough. To him it seems to be a symptom of immediate dissolution; and, indeed, if a remedy be not speedily applied, a break is the certain and not distant consequence. Fortunately, sloughs are generally easily checked, if men and material are at hand, though it is not even every experienced "high-water fighter" who knows how to handle them. Briefly, the treatment is based on the aphorism previously laid down, that wet earth is as good as dry, if it can only be made to preserve its form. What is first desired is then to arrest the movement of the sloughing earth and hold it in place. Now it does not take a great deal of force to accomplish this. If the ground at the base of the levee be tolerably hard and sound, stakes may be driven either in one row or in two braced together, according to the gravity of the case, and saplings or rails or plank laid longitudinally against them, so as to form a mechanical obstruction to the further sliding of the earth. If the ground be unsound or soft, a weight must be made to answer the same purpose as the stakes. The base of the sloughing portion must be covered with a thick layer of brush and earth placed upon it in sufficient quantity to arrest the movement. Next, to replace the loss of the sloughed material the same process is repeated; that is, brush is laid upon the damaged slope and covered with earth. The brush in these cases answers a two-fold purpose. It keeps the new and dry earth from intermixing with the old and wet and thus adding to the quagmire, and it allows the water which is percolating through the levee to run off through its interstices instead of remaining to form pools and soften the new and sound earth.

This treatment of sloughs has been practiced for a long time in Mississippi, but it seems not to be generally known in Louisiana. It is expeditious and cheap, however, and very effective, and deserves to be generally adopted.

A fifth cause of crevasses is the sudden caving away of a portion of a levee, either causing an actual gap or so weakening the embankment that it can no longer resist the pressure. This is an accident of not very frequent occurrence, considering the tremendous rapidity with which the river sometimes makes inroads upon the friable alluvial soil. I have known a strip of land more than one thousand feet wide to be cut away in a single year, and I have seen a semi-circular bite taken out four hundred and fifty feet deep in one morning. But these danger points are well known and carefully guarded against, new levees being built back of the old, so as to replace the latter if they should cave away. Sometimes, however, the engineer is compelled, by scantiness of funds, to "take chances"—that is, he has more bad places to take care of than he has money to do it with, so he must turn his attention to those which he thinks most serious and most imminent, leaving the others to be treated hastily, in an emergency, if necessary. Occasionally, but very rarely, the engineer "gets caught" by a sudden cave, greater than usual or in an unexpected place, and a break is the result. Usually a temporary levee can be hastily thrown up, in a few days, sufficient to obviate immediate disaster, and at least give time to erect a more permanent defense.

A sixth cause of crevasses has been brought strongly into prominence during the flood just passed, and that is insecure or treacherous foundations. An embankment may be strong enough in itself to resist water for an indefinitely long time, but it may rest on a stratum of weak or porous earth. Now the material of the embankment is densely packed together, as is shown by the well-known fact that "made earth" occupies much less space than loose natural soil. Therefore, it may well be that the weak point of the whole system lies under the levee and not in it. This has long been known in the case of levees with a small base, and it is an argument the more against constructing such embankments with steeper slopes than the standard, even though of strong and tenacious earth. Suppose, for an illustration, that a levee is composed of a block of solid iron, six feet wide and twelve feet high, laid upon a stratum of pure sand, and is exposed to the external pressure of twelve feet of water. The iron will neither break, overturn nor slide, but the water, after remaining sufficiently long to penetrate and soften the soil, will force the sand out from beneath the wall, and make a breach under it. To take a less extreme case: There are soils known as "water bearing"—that is, of so little consistency that they are easily permeable by water, and allow the transmission of the pressure derived from a higher source. A stratum of this kind under a levee, even of greater dimensions than are supposed above, would propagate the pressure from the external water to the thin layer or crust of loam or clay on the land side, and force or "blow it up."

It was thought, however, that an embankment of so great a base as six or seven to one of height would be safe even though built on a very light soil, for the pressure of the water on the outside is constantly resisted by the friction which it encounters in passing through the pores of the ground, and becomes weaker and weaker as it progresses landward. The experience of past years seemed to confirm this view. In 1882 out of 159 breaks, great and small, in the levees of the Yazoo basin, all but *two* occurred from the actual overtopping of the levees by water or from breaches made by the storm of the 28th of February of that year. None, so far as I know, were attributed to weakness of foundation. Yet in 1890 the five breaks that occurred in the lower Mississippi district were all, I think, due to this cause, and the single break in the upper district may very probably be ascribed to it. The difference is that in 1882 the levees were several feet lower than in 1890, and they broke before the water had got very high. If the levees had been high enough to hold the flood for two or three weeks more, doubtless we should have had an experience more analogous to that of the present season.

To provide an absolutely secure foundation in the variable soil of the Mississippi bottom without incurring enormous and ruinous expense seems almost impracticable. Yet resort may be had to expedients that promise a practical assurance of safety. It has long been customary among levee builders, before commencing the construction of the embankment, to dig a ditch three or four feet deep parallel to the general line of the levee and to fill it with well tamped clay or strong loam. Such a trench is called a "muck ditch." By some etymologists this is supposed to be a corruption of "mock ditch," but I am not aware of any evidence to support the hypothesis. Usually the dimensions given to this feature have been insignificant and its effect correspondingly small. It might, however, be rendered an important safeguard by making it six or eight feet deep and correspondingly wide and paying especial attention to the tamping, thus increasing the length of the route to be traveled by the percolating water, and by giving additional height and weight to the column of mixed earth and water that has to sustain, on the land side, the upward pressure proceeding from the weight of the external water. Given a levee ten feet high, with no muck ditch, and a water-bearing stratum two feet below the surface, we have a pressure of ten feet of water on the outside with only a weight of two feet of earth to offset it. But put a foundation of six additional feet beneath this levee, and we have sixteen feet of water offset by eight of earth, which is much better. Moreover, twelve feet more of frictional resistance have been introduced. Other important auxiliaries are increased width of berme on the outside and a banquette, as it is called, on the inside, this latter being a layer of "made earth" three or four feet deep and twenty or thirty feet wide, intended to give additional security against sloughing and to hold down by its weight the internal crust and keep it from "blowing up."

It is much easier to prevent a break than to close it after it has once occurred. This is, in fact, a task which is sometimes so beset with difficulties as to be impossible with ordinary means and in a limited time. The circumstances which determine the degree of difficulty are the height of the levee broken, the length of the crevasse, the quality of the soil and the abundance and scarcity of material. The processes of closing breaks are different in minor details, but the basis of them all is pile-work, forming a skeleton structure, more or less complete and strong, supplemented with sheet-piling or sacks, or both. In any case a great quantity of earth is requisite. Usually, within a few hours after the occurrence of the break, everything is covered with water, so that earth is to be obtained only from the body of the levee itself. In the case of a long and deep break it is easy to see what trouble would be experienced in securing a sufficiency of earth—it would involve the robbing of the levee perhaps for miles—and that, too, where the quantity already existing in the embankment was none too great, as shown by the occurrence of the break. The principal obstacle, however, in ordinary soils, is the *scour* prevailing in the immediate vicinity of the break, which increases tremendously with the least obstruction. It is difficult then, even with the utmost dilligence, to complete the skeleton pile-dike which is to be the basis of all our operations. As soon as contraction begins scour begins also, and many an engineer has seen a day's laborious pile-driving washed out in the succeeding night. The most signal instances of success in closing breaks have been in lower Louisiana, in the sugar region, where the soil is a stiff and waxy clay, not prone to scour. In such a soil, breaks enlarge slowly either in depth or width, and frequently attain no great magnitude, even when unchecked. Moreover, piles or earth placed in position with a view to closure, will remain a sufficient time to allow the completion of the work. In the upper part of the Mississippi valley a great break has never been closed except after the partial recession of the flood.

There are many topics of great interest and importance to the levee engineer which cannot now be touched on. A word of explanation may, however, be necessary in regard to the continual increase in the height of levees, which has been more than once alluded to. This is not by any means due, as is sometimes vulgarly supposed, to a rise of the bed of the river, nor even to any greater frequency or height of floods, but principally to two causes—first, to the much closer confinement of the waters which now exists, and which is marching toward perfection with great strides every year, and second, to the caving away of the original high alluvial bank of the river, and its consequent recession to the lower grounds, whereby it happens that when a levee caves away and has to be replaced by a new one, the latter must be built on ground perhaps three or four feet lower than before. Thus it has happened that where in 1874 a levee four or five feet high sufficed, there is now one which averages seventeen, but it is a mile and a-half back of the site of the former one. Its top is not much higher than before, but its bottom is ten feet lower.

THE MISSISSIPPI RIVER.

THE CONSTITUTIONAL POWER OF CONGRESS TO MAKE APPROPRIATIONS TO RESTRAIN ITS FLOOD WATERS, AS WELL AS TO IMPROVE ITS NAVIGATION—THE OBLIGATION OF THE FEDERAL GOVERNMENT TO DO BOTH.

HON. N. C. BLANCHARD, M. C., La.

[NOTE.—Owing to press of duties, Mr. Blanchard was not able to arrange this article on a basis different from the results of his study and research into the questions with which it deals, as expressed in his speeches in the House of Representatives of the United States. His treatment of the question won him enconiums from the whole country, and is truly a masterly and an ingenious legal argument.—ED.]

The great Mississippi river has a way, periodically, of overflowing its banks, to the great destruction of property of citizens, and in many instances the destruction of human lives. It is time that the country—time that the Congress of the United States—should wake up to the idea that something must be done to harness the great river in order that it may afford, not only a safe highway to the commerce and trade of the country, but that there may be a safe and easy passage of its waters to the Gulf. The time has come for the popular sentiment of the country to make itself heard and felt in support of the proposition that the Government of the United States ought to lend its helping hand, not only in the line of the improvement of the channel navigation of the river, but also to control the river with respect to preventing its floods. The Mississippi river is the great sewer of our country. It drains the waters that fall upon more than twenty-five States of this Union. Even the rain that falls upon the western portion of the great Empire State of New York finds its way to the Gulf of Mexico through the soil of Louisiana. Steamboats have penetrated as far as the town of Olean, in the State of New York, away up on the Alleghany river, which in turn pours into the Ohio, which in turn empties into the Mississippi, and then into the Gulf. And far from that point, away to the westward, far beyond Fort Benton in Montana, or to the tops of the Rocky Mountains—this great drainage basin extends. From the Canadian line on the north to the sun-kissed waves of the Mexican gulf on the south, the rainfall of nearly one-half the entire northern portion of the American continent finds its way through the State of Louisiana to the sea.

The Mississippi river is too great a national feature of our country to be handled by any State or aggregation of States. No other power than that of the National Government is potential enough to take it in hand and make it perform its twofold function of affording a national highway for the commerce of the Republic and of discharging its flood-waters safely into the Gulf of Mexico. If this river drained any one of the great nations of Europe it would long since have had dikes or levees erected along its banks of sufficient height and strength to restrain its floods.

The river is the property of the Federal Government. It is its property in the sense that its jurisdiction over it is paramount to that of the States which border upon it. The States can not say what shall be done with the river or to it, nor how it shall be treated. They are not permitted to divert it or change its course, nor to injure or interfere with its navigation.

Suppose Congress should withhold its hand and its money, and do nothing towards restraining the flood waters of the river and preventing inundations. In default of such action by the General Government the right of self-preservation arises, and the States and individuals in the valley are themselves entitled to take the matter in hand and resort to such means as they may devise to control the flood discharge of the river for their own protection and for the protection of their property. Suppose, then, that the dwellers in the lower valley of the river, despairing of Congressional action, should resort to the plan of opening innumerable outlets all along the line of the river in every direction available, on the idea advanced by some, but denied by me, that outlets might contribute to preventing disastrous floods. They might so dissipate and scatter the waters of the river by means of these outlets that the navigable character of the great stream might be seriously impaired, if not entirely lost or destroyed. Suppose they were attempting such a thing, would not the strong arm of the Federal Government be extended to prevent it? Would not Congress say, "You shall not construct works or so treat the Mississippi river as to destroy its navigable character?" Undoubtedly. When Mr. Jefferson acquired the territory known as Louisiana from France the great and controlling idea actuating that acquisition was that the American Union should control the territory through which flows the Mississippi river, in order that the river might be forever open as a great highway for the commerce of the world .

The United States, then, is interested in preserving the navigable character of the river, and must necessarily check, by legislation or other means, the construction of works that may be designed to destroy, or which might have the effect of destroying its navigation. But could the government do this without, in justice and fairness, assuming the obligation itself of so curbing and restraining the river as to give a safe and easy discharge of its flood waters? The question admits of but one answer. It could not.

What the Federal Government has heretofore done, in respect to appropriations for the Mississippi river, has been based entirely upon the idea that the money must be used exclusively for the channel improvement of the river. The government has not expended a dollar except upon the idea that the improvement of the navigation of the river was the direct object. It is true that some $3,000,000 have been expended in ten years by the Mississippi River Commission in co-operation with the States and levee boards in levee building, but it has been upon the idea, held by a majority of the river commission, that levee building, which means artificial walls to trail down the flood waters of the river between, are necessary adjuncts to channel improvement. It is time for Congress to go a step further; not only to appropriate money for the purpose of improving the navigation of the river, but also directly for the purpose of preventing its floods.

Appropriations made by Congress for this river should not be limited and restricted to works essential alone for the channel navigation of the river. Congress ought to be generous and liberal enough to go further and make appropriations for the lower river, from Cairo to the Gulf, for the object of preventing floods as well as of improving navigation. It has been doubted in many quarters that there is constitutional authority in Congress to do this. The constitutional authority to appropriate money for purposes of the channel improvement of the river to benefit navigation, is not denied under the power in the Constitution to regulate commerce; but it is denied by some that there is any warrant in the Constitution for Congress to go further and appropriate money for the direct purpose of restraining the flood waters of the river.

The money heretofore expended on the river for the purpose of levee building to restrain the floods, has been based entirely upon the idea, as I have said, that levee building is a necessary adjunct to channel improvement. But the restrictive clauses, always attached to the appropriation for the lower Mississippi river, have fettered the operations of the Mississippi River Commission and prevent them from going as far as they otherwise would go in levee building, especially at points along the river where levee construction might have no bearing upon channel improvement, but which was necessary and desirable to prevent inundation.

While somewhat of a strict constructionist of the Constitution, I have no trouble in deducing authority from that instrument justifying Congress in appropriating money for the twofold purpose of improving the navigation of the river and of restraining its flood waters.

A complete levee system is the only means of restraining the flood waters of the river. The trouble with the present levees on the river is that they have not been constructed under any general and continuous system. The Federal Government alone has the power and means to do this. The present levees have been built by piecemeal by the States, local levee boards, and individuals, as best they could.

The people of the State of Louisiana tax themselves in two ways to build levees—one is by a direct State tax, the money raised from which is disbursed under the authority of the State government; the other by a levee district tax. Under the constitution of Louisiana the Legislature of the State is authorized to subdivide the alluvial parts of the State into levee districts with taxing power, and that has been done. Each of these districts levies a tax upon all the taxable property within its limits, and the money thus raised is expended in constructing or repairing levees by the district levee boards. But the State and levee district boards are confined to the territorial limits of the State. They cannot go beyond the limits of the State, into the States north of us, and continue the system of levees, even if they had the means to do so. The State of Arkansas, up to a recent date, had no levee districts, and no tax was levied in that State generally for the construction and repair of levees. In the State of Mississippi they have levee taxing districts. But the moneys raised by Louisiana and Mississippi and their levee district boards are not expended on a continuous and connected system of levees constructed on scientific principles, and no power can undertake the construction of such a connected systematic line of levees except the Government of the United States. Hence the necessity and advisability of the Government of the United States undertaking the work.

I have stated that there was ample constitutional authority for Congress to do this. Let us now examine a little into that question.

An enemy invades us. Our people fly to arms. Points of defense are strengthened. The eye of strategy selects other points to be fortified and defended. Congress votes the money and immediately long lines of breastworks guard our frontier where attack is apprehended.

But here is an enemy who comes in the form of raging waters, sweeping down in resistless might from the North upon the sunny valleys of the West and South, bringing devastation, destruction, death. He raids through the country, rioting in ruin; and millions, panic-stricken, flee at his approach, leaving their all to be swallowed up in the wild vortex of destruction. The wasting presence lasts but a couple of months, but in that time there has been a destruction of property, present and prospective, equal in value to many millions of dollars.

It is the duty of Congress to say to these people who have so often experienced the disasters of inundation that, even as we would erect breastworks on our frontier to repel the threatened invasion of a warlike foe, so will we build levees along the great river to beat back its surging waters, threatening destruction well-nigh equal to what a human enemy could inflict.

But, it may be argued, the delegation of power to Congress to "repel invasions," "to protect the States against invasion," has reference to a human foe. I grant that that is the usual and ordinary meaning or significance given to the term, and it is likely that the framers of the Constitution had in contemplation a human foe when they inserted that clause. The connection, too, in which it is used gives additional weight to that argument. But still, the power conferred by the words "repel invasions," by the clause "The United States * * * shall protect each of them (the States) against invasion," is a general one, and might well and reasonably include defending the country against danger or harm of any kind.

Suppose some monster, like the fabled dragon of ancient times, were to rise up out of the deep and invade the land, spreading devastation, destruction, pestilence and death around him. Does any one doubt the constitutional power and duty of Congress to "repel" his invasion, to bring the strong arm of the government to bear against him, to make war upon and kill and destroy him? I think not. And yet, sir, there are gentlemen on this floor who deny to Congress the power to "repel" the invasion of waters, to throttle this monster of inundation whose periodical visitation of the fairest portion of our country is but the recurring occasion for a perfect carnival of waste, ruin, rapine.

It is the duty of Congress to protect the States, or any one of them, against invasion. By "invasion" is meant against harm or danger to the government, the people, the country, threatened by an enemy. An enemy is only to be dreaded because of the suffering, destruction, death he may inflict. Judged by that standard, was not the recent great overflow in the alluvial basin of the Mississippi "an enemy?" None will deny its potency as an engine of suffering, destruction and death. Why, then, cannot Congress under this clause of the Constitution protect the Valley States against a recurrence of this "invasion" of waters?

Again, it is made the constitutional duty of Congress to protect each of the States, under certain conditions, against "domestic violence." Why not against the violence of domestic waters? I say "domestic waters" for the reason that it is a fact that all the water which seeks an outlet to the sea through the Mississippi is the drainage of the territory of the United States, and in that sense is domestic, as pertaining to home; not foreign.

REGULATING THE PROPERTY OF THE UNITED STATES.

The Constitution (Article IV, section 3) provides:

That Congress shall have power to dispose of and make all needful rules and regulations respecting the territory or other property belonging to the United States.

In the Gratiot case (14 Peters, 537) the Supreme Court of the United States, construing the above clause, said:

The term "territory," as here used, is merely descriptive of one kind of property, and is equivalent to the word "lands." And Congress has the same power over it as over any other property belonging to the United States; and this power is vested in Congress without limitation.

In the case of McCulloch *vs.* Maryland (4 Wheaton, 422) the Chief Justice, as the organ of the court, speaking of this clause of the Constitution and the powers of Congress growing out of it, applies it to Territorial Governments, and says all admit their constitutionality.

Story says (volume 2, page 228):

No one has ever doubted the authority of Congress to erect Territorial governments within the territory of the United States, under the general language of the clause "to make all needful rules and regulations."

He continues:

The power is not confined to the territory of the United States, but extends to "other property belonging to the United States;" so that it may be applied to the due regulation of all other personal and real property rightfully belonging to the United States. And so it has been constantly understood and acted on.

Now, then, if the Mississippi is the property of the

general government, it is as much subject to "regulation" as the landed property or territory of the United States. And this power to regulate includes curbing, controlling, restraining the river within its own proper metes and bounds by means of levees, dikes or other works, as Congress may, in its discretion, see proper to adopt; for, in the language of the Gratiot case, "this power is vested in Congress without limitation."

But it may be denied that the Mississippi river is the property of the United States in the sense that Congress may, under the power to regulate, direct the construction of works to restrain its waters within their proper channel. The Mississippi river is a great national highway.

It belongs as much to the United States as would a great trunk line of railroad that had been constructed, stocked and was being operated by the government. In the act of Congress enabling the people of Louisiana to form a constitution there is a provision that the State convention shall "pass an ordinance providing that the river Mississippi and the navigable rivers and waters leading into the same or into the Gulf of Mexico shall be common highways and forever free, as well to the inhabitants of the said State as to other citizens of the United States." And in the act for the admission of Louisiana the above provision as to the navigation of the Mississippi is made one of the fundamental conditions of the admission. Similar conditions were likewise imposed upon the admission of the States of Mississippi, Missouri and Arkansas.

In the case of The United States *vs.* The New Bedford Bridge (Woodbury & Minot's Reports, 421), Mr. Justice Woodbury used the following language:

For purposes of foreign commerce and of that from State to State, the navigable rivers of the whole country seem to me to be within the jurisdiction of the general government, with all the powers over them for such purposes (whenever they choose to exercise them) which existed previously in the States or now exist with Parliament in England.

In the case of Corfield *vs.* Coryell (4 Washington Circuit Court Reports, 379), Mr. Justice Washington said:

The grant to Congress to regulate commerce on the navigable waters belonging to the several States renders those waters the public property of the United States for all purposes of navigation and commercial intercourse, subject only to Congressional regulation.

And in the case of Gilman *vs.* Philadelphia (3 Wallace, 724), it was said:

The power to regulate commerce comprehends the control for that purpose, and to the extent necessary, of all the navigable waters of the United States which are accessible from a State other than those in which they lie. For this purpose they are the public property of the nation, and subject to all the requisite legislation of Congress. This necessarily includes the power to keep them open and free from any obstruction to their navigation, interposed by the States or otherwise; to remove such obstructions when they exist, and to provide by such sanctions as they may deem proper against the recurrence of the evil, and for the punishment of offenders. For these purposes Congress possesses all the powers which existed in the States before the adoption of the national Constitution, and which have always existed in the Parliament in England. It is for Congress to determine when its full power shall be brought into activity, and as to the regulations and sanctions which shall be provided.

It can not, therefore, be doubted that the river, for all practical purposes, is the property of the General Government and subject to its "regulation," whether as respects prescribing rules for governing the commerce and traffic which make use of it as a highway, or as respects controlling it in the sense of denying the dominion and jurisdiction of the States, or other powers; or as respects preventing the river from rising up out of its customary channel and spreading over the country. It is true, the banks of the river and soil under the river belong respectively to the owners of the soil adjacent to the river, but no one will deny to the General Government the right to make use of the banks and soil in the erection of the works requisite to the proper "regulation" of the river for all useful purposes. Should, however, this right be questioned there can be no doubt of the power of the Government in the exercise of the prerogative of eminent domain, to expropriate whatever may be needed for the proper "regulation" of the river.

The law on this subject is universally recognized, as laid down by Bynkershoek, that "this eminent domain may be lawfully exercised whenever public necessity or public utility requires it."

It may be objected by some that should the Federal Government provide the ways and means for the construction of a levee system for the protection of the alluvial valley of the river, and as an adjunct to the improvement of its navigation, inasmuch as these levees will have to be constructed on the banks over which the jurisdiction of the States respectively extend, contention may arise between the State government and the National Government on this point; that the State government might deny the right of the National Government to control the levees, to protect them after constructing them, and that the question thus raised may become a fruitful source of trouble between the sovereignty vested in the State and that reposing in the Federal Government.

I am not one of those who apprehend that any trouble on this score would ever arise, but as a precautionary measure Congress might, if it sees fit, after having determined upon a levee system, enact that there should be no expenditure of money for such purposes within the territorial limits of a State until the State shall have ceded to the National Government the right to control and protect the public works to be constructed.

The State which I have the honor to represent in part in the Congress of the United States has already led off in that direction. In the constitutional convention of Louisiana which convened in 1879, and which framed the organic law under which that State is now governed, I, as a member of the convention, and as chairman of its committee on Federal relations, acting on the suggestion of Hon. E. W. Robertson, then a Representative in Congress from the Sixth district of Louisiana, and chairman of the Committee on Levees and Improvements of the Mississippi of the House, reported to the convention the following ordinance, which was adopted, and now stands as part of article 215 of the constitution of 1879 of Louisiana, to wit:

> The Federal Government is authorized to make such geological, topographical, hydrographical, and hydrometrical surveys and investigations within the State as may be necessary to carry into effect the act of Congress to provide for the appointment of a Mississippi River Commission for the improvement of said river from the Head of the Passes near its mouth to the headwaters, and to construct and protect such public works and improvements as may be ordered by Congress under the provisions of said act.

Under this article full authority is given the National Government to construct such public works along the Mississippi as Congress may see fit to order, and the control of the same after their construction is ceded to the National Government.

The State of Louisiana, in incorporating this grant of authority in her organic law, recognized what is now generally conceded, namely, that there is no power competent to handle the questions presented by this great river except that of the Federal Government. No State can do it.

First. Because the work is too vast, too costly for any State through which the river runs to undertake it.

Second. Because any State attempting it would be circumscribed by its own territorial limits.

Third. Because the river being the property of the United States, Congress alone has power, under the grant to "make all needful rules and regulations respecting the territory or other property belonging to the United States," to say what works shall be done or plans adopted for its regulation.

POST-OFFICES AND POST-ROADS.

Under the authority "to establish post-offices and post-roads" the Government of the United States has established thousands of the former in the alluvial valleys of the Mississippi and its tributaries, and provided a perfect network of the latter. Daily over thousands of miles of roadway and railway and water way in the great valley is the United States mail carried, supplying innumerable postoffices and affording facilities indispensable for the dissemination of intelligence, for the diffusion of the market reports, the crop and commercial reports, and the news generally so absolutely needed for the welfare, the happiness and the prosperity of the people and the country.

Millions of money, besides great labor and much valuable time, have been expended in building up and perfecting this system, which in the normal state of the country moves with the precision, ease and regularity of well-ordered machinery. But periodically the great river swells up out of its banks and becomes a great inland sea, producing an abnormal condition of affairs, and disarranging, stopping, destroying for the time being the postal service, the transportation and delivery of the mails.

On our statute-books, as the enactments of Congress, stand stringent penal laws denouncing penalties against any and all who shall willfully impede, interfere with, or stop the mails; and the courts of the United States hold sittings all over the valley to enforce these laws. But here is a great convulsion of nature, as it were, that stops not one mail but a thousand, that breaks up not one postoffice but hundreds, and against which the courts and the criminal laws for the protection and security of the mails avail nothing. But to prevent a recurrence of this is the strong arm of the Government powerless? No. Scientific, wise, experienced men, who have made a study of the river and its phenomena, of the laws of its currents, and of the conditions that affect it, say no! They have pointed out how these destructive floods can be avoided, and thus how the mails of the United States, their carriage and delivery, can be protected.

Now, then, does any one doubt that from the authority "to establish post-offices and post-roads" flows not only the power but the duty to protect them? No reasonable man can doubt it. No lawyer will hesitate for an instant to declare that the power to protect is incidental to the power to establish. The constitutionality of the laws denouncing penalties against the stoppage of, or interference with, the mails has never been doubted. Yet they were enacted for the protection of the mails, and depend for their validity upon the power to protect being incidental to the power to establish. Says the Supreme Court of the United States, in 4 Wheaton, 417:

TO ESTABLISH POST-OFFICES AND POST-ROADS.

This power is executed by the single act of making the establishment. But from this has been inferred the power and duty of carrying the mail along the post-road from one post-office to another. And from this implied power has again been inferred the right to punish those who steal letters from the post-office or rob the mail. It may be said with some plausibility, that the right to carry the mail and to punish those who rob it is not indispensably necessary to the establishment of a post-office and post-road. This right is indeed essential to the beneficial exercise of the power, but not indispensably necessary to its existence.

Yet no one doubts or denies the right or power of the government to punish the robber of the mails. Now, then, is it not just as legitimate, just as constitutional, to protect against the ravages of water as against the knavery of the robber?

TO REGULATE COMMERCE.

The power of Congress to regulate commerce includes the regulation of intercourse and navigation. (18 Howard, 421.)

Says Story, volume 2, page 4:

Commerce undoubtedly is traffic; but it is something more. It is intercourse. It describes the commercial intercourse between nations and parts of nations in all its branches, and is regulated by prescribing rules for carrying on that intercourse.

This power to regulate commerce is a very general one, and a wide latitude of construction has been given it.

If a levee system tends, in any appreciable degree, to afford ease and safety to commerce, to intercourse, which is essential to the carrying on of commerce, then an appropriation of money by Congress to construct such a system finds abundant justification in this grant of power.

The Mississippi River Commission, in their report of February 17, 1880, say regarding levees:

There is no doubt that the levees exert a direct action in deepening the channel and enlarging the bed of the river during those periods of "rise" and "flood" when, by preventing the dispersion of the flood-waters over the adjacent lowlands, either over the river banks or through bayous and other openings, they actually cause the river to rise to a higher level within the river-bed than it would attain if not thus restrained. * *. *

They give safety and ease to navigation, and promote and facilitate commerce and trade by establishing banks or landing-places above the reach of floods, upon which produce can be placed while awaiting shipment and where steamboats and other craft can land in time of high water. * * * In a larger sense, as embracing not only beneficial effects upon the channel but a protection against destructive floods, a levee system is essential, and such a system also promotes and facilitates commerce, trade, and the postal service.

To the same effect are the subsequent reports of the commission and the statements of the individual members thereof before the committees of Congress.

Prior to the act creating this commission a board of engineers was appointed on the improvement of the low-water navigation of the river below Cairo, Ill. In their report to the Chief of Engineers, dated January 25, 1879, on the "effect of a permanent levee system on the Mississippi below the mouth of the Ohio river," they say:

To deal with the question whether there is any connection between levees and facilities for shipping, commerce and navigation at high stages, we refer to the actual condition of things. We find that throughout all the extension of the Mississippi along which the levee system is practically efficient, and where the marginal lands are generally cleared and cultivated, the levees have been an important aid to commerce. * * * Below the mouth of the Arkansas, as far down as the forts below New Orleans, the levees have been long enough in existence to give evidence of their effect, direct and indirect. Immediately behind them are the cultivated lands, the plantations whence comes sugar, cotton and other valuable staples. To each one of these plantations not only is the levee the protecting agent which renders their cultivation practicable, but it is during floods the landing-place of the steamboats, barges, or flat boats which bring their supplies and carry their productions away. * * * *

In the lower river, through the regions where the margins are under cultivation, the levees are generally laid close to these margins and afford, as has already been stated, useful facilities for commerce in making practicable the coming alongside of steamers and the receiving of the products of the plantations and discharging freights for the use of the same or for the back country. In ordinary rises the natural banks are not overflowed, but when that happens in "flood" years they, (the levees) serve a purpose in still defining the channel.

From testimony like this it can not be doubted that levees aid not only in improving the navigation of the river, but are themselves factors in the giving of ease and safety to commercial intercourse.

If the Federal Government can legitimately spend millions in affording facilities to commerce by improving the low-water navigation of rivers, by parity of reasoning it may just as legitimately spend millions in improving the high-water navigation of rivers like the Mississippi, liable to overflow their banks. And the weight of evidence ten times over is that for the Mississippi and its tributaries a levee system is the most efficient method of improving their high-water navigation.

By the navigation of rivers is meant not alone the passage of steamers and other craft up and down, but in a larger sense it includes likewise facilities for landing along the rivers for the loading and unloading of cargoes, the taking on and putting off of passengers, etc. In other words, it embraces the affording of all needful facilities for intercourse, trade, traffic, and commerce, besides the width, depth, and extent of water requisite for the safe passage of boats.

Again, navigation is only one of the elements of commerce. It is an element of commerce because it affords the means of transporting merchandise and the products of the country, the interchange of which is commerce itself. The river is but an instrument of commerce.

The power to regulate commerce is a power to regulate the instruments of commerce. (Gray *vs*. Clinton Bridge, 16 American Law Register, 152.)

It extends to the persons who conduct it as well as to the instruments used. (Cooley *vs*. Board of Wardens, 12 Howard, 316.

The commerce of the river and the commerce across the river are both commerce among the States, and may be regulated by Congress, and should be regulated by that body when any regulation is necessary. (16 American Law Register, 154.)

It is now conceded that Congress, under the commercial clause, may regulate railroads. May it not, also regulate the Mississippi, a national highway and an instrument which commerce makes use of, so as to prevent it disturbing the commerce and intercourse going on by rail and by land in its valley?

The term "to regulate commerce" gives the power to restrain the destructive force of the thing used by commerce in its transactions. It is an incongruity to say that Congress, in the exercise of that power, may deepen or enlarge a river but can not curb its force or exercise restraint over it.

The power "to regulate commerce" necessarily includes protection to commerce. This idea has been acted on from the commencement of the government. The construction and maintenance all along our coasts of light-houses, beacon-lights, fog-signals, sea-walls, and break-waters attest this. All are for the protection and convenience of commerce.

The laws of the United States require steam-vessels to pay for the license or privilege to navigate, and the officers manning such vessels are required to pay for the license or privilege of pursuing their respective calling or vocation, such as master, pilot, mate, etc. These vessels engage in the coasting trade as well as in the carrying trade, and Congress is as much under obligation to afford the needful facilities for the transaction of this coasting trade as it is for the transportation of through freights. One of the facilities needed along the Mississippi for the coasting trade is convenient landing-places at all times.

In seasons of flood, these landing-places are supplied

by the levees, and, in this season, levees are but continuing piers or quays. A quay is defined to be a space of ground appropriated to the public use, such use as the convenience of commerce requires. Now, while the levees perform this service, while they furnish these needed conveniences to commerce, should it be objected that, at the same time, they protect the country behind them from overflow? Suppose they do protect private property while performing a public service, should they not be commended all the more for that? Should not that circumstance really be an additional inducement or argument for their construction?

Should not broad and liberal statesmanship, in considering a question of this sort, rather approve of a system which, while subserving the public interests, at the same time affords needed protection to the life and property of the individual? *Salus populi suprema lex.* Protection to private property in some way results from nearly every work of public import. If a street in a town or city be graded, paved or macadamized, the property belonging to individuals on that street experience an enhancement of value as the result of such improvement.

Every railroad constructed through a country increases the value of the lands adjacent thereto. Every grand, imposing public building erected in this city (Washington), and every park laid out, beautified, adorned, adds something to the worth of neighboring private estates.

This question of regulating the Mississippi certainly comes within the general police power of the government, under which power "persons and property are subjected to all kinds of restraint and burdens in order to secure the general comfort, health and prosperity of the state." (27 Vt., 149; quoted approvingly in 5 Otto, 471.) In the latter case the Supreme Court, speaking of the deposit in Congress of the power to regulate commerce, say:

What that power is it is difficult to define with sharp precision. It is generally said to extend to making regulations promotive of domestic order, morals, health, and safety. As was said in Thorp vs. The Rutland and Burlington Railroad Company, 27 Vt., 149, it extends to the protection of the lives, limbs, health, comfort and quiet of all persons, and the protection of all property within the state. According to the maxim, *Sic utere tuo ut alienum non lædas*, which, being of universal application, it must of course be within the range of legislative action to define the mode and manner in which every one may so use his own as not to injure others.

If the government fails to exercise its police powers to control its property, and this property, like a great river, rises and inundates the country, and great damage to individuals results, the government is, or ought to be responsible.

Take the case of an Indian tribe placed by the government upon a reservation, and over which it exercises jurisdiction and surveilance. From some cause an outbreak occurs. The Indians throw off the restraint they are under, band themselves together, commence hostilities, and raid the surrounding country. For the damage and loss occasioned individuals by such an outbreak the government has repeatedly acknowledged its liability, and Congress has over and over again appropriated money to make good such losses.

Now, why should it not be equally responsible for losses occasioned by the Mississippi when it, in time of flood, raids the adjacent country? The government not only assumes paramount jurisdiction over the river, but asserts a proprietary interest in and to it.

Why, then, should it not be under obligations to restrain and control it, equal to the restraint and control it admits it should exercise over an Indian tribe placed by it upon a reservation?

If a railroad train kills the stock of a man a suit lies to enforce payment of the value of the stock from the company. But the great Mississippi rises, and, by the neglect of the government to protect its banks by dikes, overflows, causing the destructions of millions in value of property. No suit against the Government can be filed, for this great and free Republic does not permit what the veriest despotisms of foreign lands allow, namely, the general right to its citizens to sue the Government in any court of competent jurisdiction for injuries sustained by the act of commission or omission of the Government.

The first clause of section 8, article I, of the Constitution prescribed that "Congress shall have power to lay and collect taxes, duties, imposts, and excises, to pay the debts and provide for the common defense and general welfare of the United States."

I agree with the interpretation that the above clause was not intended to invest Congress with the independent and general power "to provide for the general welfare;" and that the latter part of the clause, to wit, "to pay the debts and provide for the common defense and general welfare," is but a modification or qualification of the preceding part, namely, "Congress shall have power to lay and collect taxes," etc.

Nothing more was granted by that part ("to pay the debts and provide for the common defense and general welfare") than a power to appropriate the public money raised under the other part, ("to lay taxes,") etc.

Said Thomas Jefferson:

To lay taxes to provide for the general welfare of the United States is to lay taxes for the purpose of providing for the general welfare. For the laying of taxes is the power and the general welfare the purpose for which the power is to be exercised. Congress are not to lay taxes *ad libitum* for any purpose they please; but only to pay debts, or provide for the welfare of the Union.

Under this interpretation, while a general power to legislate for the "general welfare" is excluded, Congress is still authorized to provide money for the common defense and general welfare, and this is quite broad enough for the practical purpose we have in view. Indeed, the power to lay taxes is in express terms given to provide for the common defense and general welfare. And, as laid down by Story:

It is not pretended that when the tax is laid the specific objects for which it is laid are to be specified, or that it is to be solely applied to those objects.

It suffices that all taxes must generally be laid for one or all of three purposes, namely, to pay the debts, to provide for the common defense, or the general welfare. And when the money has accumulated in the Treasury, from taxes laid for any or all of these purposes, as said by President Monroe in his message of May 4, 1822:

The power of appropriation of the moneys [by Congress] is coextensive; that is, it may be appropriated to any purpose of the common defense and general welfare.

In other words, if operating under the latter clause, the taxes laid must be applied to some particular measure conducive to the general welfare. Or, as laid down by Story, volume 2, page 162:

The only limitations upon the power [to appropriate money in aid of internal improvements] are those prescribed by the terms of the Constitution, that the objects shall be for the common defense, or the general welfare of the Union.

The true test is whether the object be of a local character and local use, or whether it be of general benefit to the States. If it be purely local Congress can not constitutionally appropriate money for the object. But if the benefit be general it matters not whether in point of locality it be in one State or several, whether it be of large or of small extent; its nature and character determine the right, and Congress may appropriate money in aid of it, for it is then in a just sense for the general welfare.

It is not only right, but the bounden and solemn duty of Congress to advance the safety, happiness and prosperity of the people, and to provide for the general welfare by any and every act of legislation within constitutional limits, which it may deem to be conducive to those ends. No one will have the temerity to question the proposition that the protection of the extensive alluvial valley of the Mississippi from destructive floods will be, in the national sense of that term, conducive to the general welfare. Not one State, but a dozen; not a few thousand people, but millions are directly interested and affected for weal or woe according as this protection is extended or withheld. One overflow, as hereinbefore stated, has caused the destruction of many million dollars' worth of property, without taking into consideration the human and animal suffering and death inflicted by it. Does any sane man doubt that providing against the recurrence of such a public calamity is promoting the general welfare?

But it is unnecessary to dwell upon this. The point is conceded. No man of reflection will gainsay that if it were to the general welfare that we should acquire this territory, as we did, from France, it is equally conducive to the general welfare to preserve it as a habitable, cultivable country; to protect it against relegation to its primeval condition of jungles and swamps. The words of Chief-Justice Bigelow, of Massachusetts, in the case of Talbott *vs.* Hudson, 24 Law Reports, 228, are here singularly appropriate:

In a broad and comprehensive view * * * everything which tends to enlarge the resources, increase the industrial energies, and promote the productive power of any considerable number of the inhabitants of a section of the State [Union], or which leads to the growth of towns and the creation of new sources for the employment of private capital and labor, indirectly contributes to the general welfare and to the prosperity of the whole community.

Congress has exercised, not without question, it is true, but long enough for acquiescence to take place, the power to lay taxes to protect and encourage domestic manufactures.

This has been and is being done, on the ground that it is conducive to the general welfare to protect and encourage domestic manufacturers. But it is not one whit more conducive to the general welfare, if as much so, than protecting the finest portion of our country for cultivable purposes is.

All must admit that the powers of the Government are limited and that its limits are not to be transcended. But, as was observed by the Supreme Court of the United States in 4 Wheaton, 421, the sound construction of the Constitution must allow the National Legislature that discretion, with respect to the means by which the powers it confers are to be carried into execution, which will enable that body to perform the high duties assigned to it in the manner most beneficial to the people.

Let the end be legitimate, let it be within the scope of the Constitution, and all means which are appropriate, which are plainly adapted to that end, which are not prohibited, but consist with the letter and spirit of the Constitution, are constitutional.—*Ib*.

In McCulloch *vs*. Maryland (4 Wheaton, 415) Chief-Justice Marshall aptly referred to the Constitution as "intended to endure for ages to come, and consequently to be adapted to the various crisis of human affairs."

And in Hunter *vs*. Martin (1 Wheaton, 304) it was said:

The instrument (Constitution) was not intended to provide merely for the exigencies of a few years, but was to endure through a long lapse of ages, the events of which were locked up in the inscrutable purposes of Providence. It could not be foreseen what new changes and modifications of power might be indispensable to effectuate the general objects of the charter. * * * Hence its powers are expressed in general terms, leaving the Legislature, from time to time, to adopt its own means to effectuate legitimate objects, and to mold and model the exercise of its powers as its own wisdom and the public interests should require.

Then the great Father of Waters, unhindered by an adequate levee system, rises out of its banks and sweeps with resistless might over the valley, a more than crisis, a sad realization of the worst, is upon the people of that unhappy section, and this grievous affliction of one of the members of the body-politic in more or less degree disastrously affects the whole. Against the recurrence of the like calamity, national in its effect, we ask the aid of the National Government. We hold that the powers delegated in general terms in the Constitution are broad and comprehensive enough to justify it, that the granting of national aid for such purpose is directly in the line of the effectuation of the legitimate objects of the charter.

Says Story (volume 1, page 655):

Constitutions of government are not to be framed upon a calculation of existing exigencies, but upon a combination of these with the probable exigencies of ages, according to the natural and tried course of human affairs. There ought to be a capacity to provide for future contingencies as they may happen.

That this capacity exists in the Federal Constitution no one will deny. The trials it has undergone, the tests it has been put to and triumphantly emerged from, in the hundred years of its existence, abundantly attest it. Let

Congress give another evidence of this capacity by providing against the contingency of another great overflow; let this provision be ample and unrestricted; let it meet the case.

The Mississippi River Commission unanimously declare that so far as preventing floods on the river is concerned a complete and perfect system of levees is the only method that will serve that end. They unhesitatingly condemn what is called the outlet system. This is the conclusion they have reached after years of study of the river. A year or two ago in the Senate of the United States an impromptu discussion of the plan of improvement of the Mississippi river adopted by the river commission sprang up, and it was stated by a distinguished Senator from a Southwestern State that the levee system had proven a failure not only upon the Mississippi river but also upon rivers in the Old World, and he named the river Po in Europe and the Yellow river in China. He stated that levee construction upon the banks of those rivers, maintained for long periods of time, had had the effect of causing the bed or bottom of the river to rise, and consequently producing more disastrous floods than before.

As regards the Po, this statement rests upon the declaration of De Prony, a European engineer of note. But his theory was completely demolished by the investigations made by Lombardini, the great Italian hydraulic engineer, who proved conclusively that the bed of the Po had not been raised at all through two centuries of levee construction and maintenance on its banks.

As respects the Yellow river, I have been unable to find any sufficient authority upon which this statement rests. A writer on China, by the name of Williams, makes mention of something of this kind, but does not support it by sufficient facts or reasoning.

Levee construction as a means of preventing floods upon rivers is of very ancient origin. Semiramis, Queen of Assyria, erected dikes along the Euphrates to prevent the lowlands from being inundated, and Nitocris faced the banks of that great river with burned bricks in order to protect the sides of the channel from abrasion.

Most of the rivers of Europe have been diked or leveed as a preventive against floods. The Po, the Rhine, the Vistula, the Arno, the Scheldt, the Meuse, and others are thus leveed, and in consequence a disastrous inundation in Europe is now a thing of rare occurrence. Some of the works on these rivers are of great magnitude. Upon the Vistula, for instance, the levees are 20 feet high and as many broad at the top. The outlet system is not resorted to in Europe as a means of preventing floods. Outlets have been tried in the silt-bearing streams of that continent and discarded. The division formerly made of the Po at Buondeno was abandoned in the year 1838.

Robinson in his "Theory of Rivers" states that in the year 1600 the waters of the Panaro, a river of nearly equal size with the Po, were joined with those of the latter, and that in 1720 another river, almost as large, the Rheno, was diverted from its former course and made to flow into the Po. In both instances much alarm was felt by the dwellers in the valley of the Po that this cumulation of waters would result in disastrous overflows. But the reverse was true. The increased volume of water and consequent increased velocity of current caused the Po to deepen and widen its channel, the liability to overflow was greatly diminished, and several extensive marshes which, prior to that time, could not be reclaimed, were drained and rendered susceptible to habitation and cultivation.

If this be true as to the rivers of Europe, why should it not be true as to the Mississippi river? All the engineers whose sphere of duty brings them in contact with the river say it is true of it.

We hear much of the proposed Lake Borgne outlet from the Mississippi river. This plan is not new. It was examined carefully by Humphreys and Abbot, two United States engineers of long experience and great capacity, who studied the physics and hydraulics of the Mississippi river in 1858, and wrote most intelligently upon it. They rejected the Lake Borgne outlet proposition as altogether inadvisable.

I quote the language of Humphreys and Abbot. Replying to Ellet, who was the earliest writer on the Mississippi river, and who advocated outlets as a means of preventing floods, they say:

> The task of criticism is always ungrateful, and if this formula had been prepared by an obscure writer it would have remained unnoticed. Coming, however, from an engineer so well known as Mr. Ellet, and furnishing, as it does, the basis upon which rest practical conclusions believed to be most erroneous and most mischievous, it can not be passed by in silence.

Then, after discussing at length the outlet theory, they say:

No further comments are necessary to prepare one to learn that the practical conclusions of Mr. Ellet in reference to protection against the inundations of the Mississippi have been proved to be erroneous by the measurements of this survey.—*Humphreys and Abbot*, edition 1876, pages 227, 228.

The same authors, while acknowledging that, theoretically, outlets of a certain kind might do a certain amount of good, declare absolutely against the practicability of outlets on the Mississippi below Cairo, in the following terms:

Enough has been said to demonstrate with all the certainty of which the subject is capable, the disastrous consequences that must follow the resort to this means of protection [outlets].—*Humphreys and Abbot*, edition 1876, page 428.

And in reference to the treatment which should be applied to the river to prevent floods, they use the following language:

RECOMMENDATIONS.

An organized levee system must be depended upon for protection against floods in the Mississippi Valley.

The preceding discussion of the different plans of protection has been so elaborate and the conclusions adopted have been so well established that little remains to be said under the head of recommendations.

It has been demonstrated that no advantage can be derived either from diverting tributaries or constructing reservoirs, and that the plans of cut-offs and of new or enlarged outlets to the Gulf are too costly and too dangerous to be attempted. The plan of levees, on the contrary, which has always recommended itself by its simplicity and its direct repayment of investments, may be relied upon for protecting all the alluvial bottom lands liable to inundation below Cape Girardeau. The work, it is true, will be extensive and costly, and will exact much more unity of action than has thus far been attained. * * * * * * *

It will be thus seen that Humphreys and Abbot declare against diverting tributaries, against constructing reservoirs, against cut-offs, and against outlets, but give to the levee system, as the means of protecting the alluvial valley from inundation, the sanction of their judgment and approval.

General Barnard, Bayley, Forshey, Albert Stein, and others who have written on the river, take the same view. Those mentioned were all accomplished engineers, with large opportunities of observation. Without exception they declared against outlets, both theoretically and practically.

Subsequently Mr. Eads added the results of his labors and great ability to the same side of the question.

Finally, the Mississippi River Commission, after most careful experiments and large experience, find themselves opposed unanimously to outlets, and in favor of controlling and confining the flood discharge to the main river or channel.

It is a hydrostatical paradox, uniformly confirmed by experience, that you do not diminish the height of the waters in great floods by lessening the quantity of water.

This is particularly true of our alluvial rivers of the South. It is, of course, acknowledged that the first effect of the withdrawal from the river, with a fall into an open basin of a considerable part of its volume, will be to produce a lowering of its surface in the vicinity of the outlet. But the systematic improvement of the river and its treatment to prevent floods must be conducted with an intelligent knowledge of and reference to ultimate results. The ultimate result of diverting a considerable portion of the volume of water from the river is to increase its surface level.

At best, the relief that an outlet would give would be only local and temporary; local, as certainly not exceeding anywhere two or three feet, and not extending over a hundred miles of river above the outlet; and temporary, since the inexorable law of the river would surely in a very few years re-establish the adjustment between discharge, resistance, and slope.

Every break of the river from the main channel causes a lessening of the velocity of the current at and below the outlet, and this decrease of velocity causes a precipitation of sediment or silt in the bottom of the river. No greater uniformity and certainty has marked the results of any of the observations of the Mississippi River Commission than in the decrease of river section below an outlet, and, *vice versa*, its enlargement when the outlet is closed and the former regimen of the river restored.

Humphreys and Abbot, it is true, disputed the proposition that, as the result of an outlet, a bar was formed immediately below the break in the bed of the river; but fuller observations since their time have established its truth. And it stands to reason that if any considerable portion of the volume of water of a silt-bearing stream is diverted from the main channel, the force of the remainder is diminished, the normal condition of the river at that point is disturbed, and the weakened current is no longer capable of bearing along the load of sand and sediment. A part of it is cast down into the bed, the section of the river is decreased, and a bar or obstruction formed.

Relative to this question of the duty of Congress to go further than they have gone in the past and make appropriations not only to improve the navigation of the river, but to prevent its disastrous floods, I wish to call attention to some utterances on this subject by gentlemen who have occupied very exalted positions in our country.

Mr. Garfield, in his letter of acceptance of the Presidential nomination of his party, July 10, 1880, made use of this language :

The wisdom of Congress should be invoked to devise some plan by which that great river shall cease to be a terror to those who dwell upon its banks, and by which its shipping may safely carry the industrial products of 25,000,000 of people.

At that time there were 25,000,000 people in the valley of the Mississippi. To-day 35,000,000 are there.

In a speech on this floor he styled the Mississippi—

The most gigantic, single, natural feature of our continent, far transcending the glory of the ancient Nile, or of any other river on the earth.

He further declared that he believed that—

one of the grandest of our material interests—one that is national in the largest material sense—is this great river and its tributaries.

And that—

the statesmanship of America must grapple with the problem of this mighty stream; that it is too vast for any State to handle; too much for any authority less than that of the nation itself to manage.

In his day Mr. Garfield urged upon Congress to make a liberal and generous appropriation for the two fold purpose of aiding the navigation of the river and preventing its floods.

President Hayes, in his message of December, 1880, speaking of the Mississippi river and its tributaries, said:

These channels of communication and interchange are the property of the nation. Its jurisdiction is paramount over their waters, and the plainest principles of public interest require their intelligent and careful supervision with a view to their protection, improvement, and the enhancement of their usefulness.

Mr. Arthur, when he was President, sent a message to Congress on April 17, 1882, in which he made use of this language:

The immense loss and widespread suffering of the people dwelling near the river—

Occasioned by the great overflow of that year—

induce me to urge upon Congress the propriety of not only making an appropriation to close the gaps in the levees occasioned by the recent floods, as recommended by the commission, but that Congress should inaugurate measures for the permanent improvement of the navigation of the river and security of the valley.

To the same general effect were the remarks of President Cleveland in a speech delivered by him at Memphis, Tenn., during the latter part of his presidential term. There can be no doubt that the Mississippi river is, in its broadest sense, a national waterway. Let Congress rise to the full conception and execution of its duty towards it, and towards the people living in its valley.

APPENDIX.

EXTRACTS OF TESTIMONY BY U. S. ARMY ENGINEERS
IN CHARGE OF MISSISSIPPI RIVER WORK.

TAKEN BEFORE THE HOUSE COMMITTEE ON LEVEE AND THE
IMPROVEMENT OF THE MISSISSIPPI RIVER.

By CAPTAIN LEACH, U. S. Army.

The CHAIRMAN (Mr. Burrows.) We will be glad to hear from you on this subject with regard to the construction of levees as a necessary adjunct to the improvement of the Mississippi river, and in your own language describe the relative value of the levees as a part of that improvement, and the necessity, if such, for their construction.

Mr. BOATNER. And I would suggest, also, Mr. Chairman, the feasibility of protecting the valley from destructive floods by means of levees.

The CHAIRMAN. That is suggested in the title of the bill.

Captain LEACH. In relation to your first inquiry, it is as a factor in the improvement of the navigation of the Mississippi river, that a levee system is absolutely necessary and demands the attention of the General Government. So far as the Government is concerned, as I apprehend its functions, the prevention of overflow is not a necessity, although desirable. The improvement of navigation seems to be a necessity. It is a charge which is committed to the General Government in the nature of affairs, and it is the avowed policy of the Government to improve the navigation, and therefore the discussion of the value of a levee system in that respect is a very important one.

The Mississippi river performs a dual function. It is the final outlet of a very extended system of inland drainage and it is also our most important avenue of inland commerce. It happens, very fortunately, that in respect to both these functions the same remedies produce useful results, for in both it is now defective. It is not as good an avenue of commerce as it ought to be by any means, neither is it as good a drain as it ought to be. If measures to make the one better were injurious to the other, the question would be complicated, if not hopeless; but it so happens that whatever may be done to make it a better drain will improve the navigation, and whatever is done to make it a more navigable stream will also increase its capacity as a drain. The reason of this unity is essentially the fact that both the discharging capacity of the channel, which determines its usefulness as a drain, and the least depth of the water flowing in it, depend, in an alluvial stream, flowing in a bed of its own formation, on the velocity of the water; and whatever permanently increases that velocity improves the stream both as a drain and as a navigable highway.

* * * * * * * * * * * *

It is necessary to operate very frequently on the highwater current as well as the low-water current. If there is anything true about what I have stated, it is that this control, to make a complete improvement of the river, must be made perfect. Partial control of the river produces a partial improvement of the river, but we want the greatest possible improvement of the river, and therefore we should have complete control, which alone will do it. Complete control can be effected only by two agencies operating together. One is a protection from caving and shifting of the present position of the natural bank of the river, and the other is extending these banks up to the highest known water level to prevent escape of the water by overflow. The first of these agencies of course is bank revetment, and the second levees. To estimate their relative value would be very difficult. They go together. Some idea can be formed of what complete improvement will be, and it is known that complete improvement will result from both these agencies operating together, but what the one or the other will produce alone, I do not believe anyone can say; but I will say this, that neither the one nor the other will alone produce complete improvement, because complete improvement means complete control, and complete control is impossible without both of these agencies.

The CHAIRMAN. This bank revetment is necessary for the control of the river at its low stage and the levees at the high-flood tide?

Captain LEACH. Yes, sir; those are their separate functions.

The CHAIRMAN. And the river must be controlled in both of these ways to produce complete improvement?

Captain LEACH. Yes, sir, it must. Of course the bank protection acts, in addition to its own especial function of control at channel-contained stages, to protect the levees also, because we would not be able to maintain them without complete bank protection.

* * * * * * * * * * * * *

Captain LEACH. My belief is that the development of contraction works will be far less than heretofore contemplated. I think the necessary control of the current will be secured by the protection of the banks and completion of the levees, and will give all the improvement possible, because developing all the force which resides in the mass of the water and its height above the sea.

* * * * * * * * * * * * *

Mr. BOATNER. You stated that you considered levees as necessary elements to the control of the river. Will you please state what effect you observed follows the escape of water through a crevasse, or through any point where there has been any levee, what the effect is upon the channel?

Captain LEACH. We have made a number of measurements, and the effect invariably observed has been a considerable filling of the channel below the point of escape. We have also observed a reverse process on the closure of some of these same crevasses recently opened and others opened before, and we have in every case observed a deepening of the channel commensurate in amount with the shoaling observed at the time of the break. We have measured both sides of it, and never failed in any case to find data on which we could found conclusions to that effect.

* * * * * * * * * * * * *

The CHAIRMAN. Is it feasible as a matter of engineering to build a system of levees throughout that length of river that will hold the flood waters ?

Captain LEACH.* Starting from the remark I made a few minutes ago about the non-necessity of constructing a range of mountains for that purpose, I will say that the amount named in this bill, nor twice, nor three times, nor any amount I can think of, will build a system of levees behind which the people can sit in idleness and watch the flood go by and which will resist the floods themselves. It is a fight, a war, between the two, and the enemy is alert and very shrewd and persistent. It is no more possible to build a system of levees which without care and attention will resist floods than it is to build a fortification which will repulse an enemy without a garrison. Whatever is done must be by a proper system of levees, re-inforced by the most incessant care and watching, especially at time of high water, and more or less in the entire year. What the people need is a line of intrenchments of which you can say, "if you come out and make a good fight, you are bound to win."

The CHAIRMAN. Then there is no engineering difficulty in building levees of sufficient height and strength to hold the flood waters?

Captain LEACH. None whatever if they are properly cared for.

The CHAIRMAN. The building can be done?

Captain LEACH. Yes, sir.

By CAPTAIN KINGMAN, U. S. Army.

The CHAIRMAN. I would be glad if you would state to the committee your opinion in reference to the construction of levees as a means of improvement of low-water navigation, and also as a means of preventing disastrous floods and overflows. State your knowledge upon that subject fully, in your own way.

Captain KINGMAN. The condition of the Mississippi river, the laws which govern its flow, the causes which operate to injure its navigable channel, and the defects from which it now suffers, as well as the means which have been adopted to correct them, have already been pretty thoroughly set forth by Captain Leach and others. These means include the construction of levees, and of revetments to prevent the caving of the bank, and of works to contract the channel. All of these are considered necessary for the purpose of improving the navigation of the river. That levees are necessary seems to me to be proved by the simple statement that in order to secure the best navigation of which the river is capable it is necessary to have complete control of the river at all stages, and particularly at those stages at which it is capable of doing the most harm or the most good. This can be secured only by the creation of artificial banks, higher than those that the forces of the river can produce, thereby causing the stream to pass down at all stages in a comparatively narrow channel. It is a well-known fact that wherever water escapes from the channel of an alluvial river at a comparatively well-defined point, as at a crevasse, that the channel is impaired in the vicinity of the break. This has been demonstrated a great many times, and particularly during the recent high water. The largest crevasse, and the one which discharged the greatest amount of water during the flood of 1890, was the one known as the Nita Crevasse, 65 miles above New Orleans. Its maximum discharge was 400,000 cubic feet per second, or one-third of the amount of water passing in the river channel, immediately above the break.

While two thirds of the water passed down to the mouth of the river, one-third escaped through the crevasse. The surveys made when the river was falling showed that the effect of the crevasse had been to diminish the effective area of cross-section about 25 per cent., that is to say, the cross-section below the crevasse was only 75 per cent. of what it had been before the break occurred, when the river was in its normal condition.

On the Mississippi river, with an incomplete system of levees, with an imperfect system, or with no system at all, we shall have at every flood a number of pretty well defined points at which a portion of the water will escape from the main channel and flow for long distances in lateral channels remote from it. Each one of these points of escape will be a center from which deterioration of the waterway will spread. This deterioration may or may not become sufficient to interfere with low-water navigation. I do not know that it has ever been sufficient to prevent it. If the escape of water is not very great the effect would probably never be observed by pilots when the break was opposite a deep portion of the river; for a reduction of depth from 100 feet to 60 feet would make no difference to them, though it would seriously impair the river as a drain. In the case of a large break, however, near a shoal portion of the river, the injurious effect could not fail to be observable on the low-water channel.

I could mention a great many cases where breaks in the levees have been injurious to navigation, and where the rebuilding of a levee has restored the former conditions. I will mention the Morganza Crevasse, a very large one, which was situated about 30 miles below the mouth of the Red river, on the right bank. The water that escaped through it never returned, but found its way to the Gulf by the way of the Atchafalaya.

Mr. CATCHINGS. I suppose that is true of the Nita Crevasse also?

Captain KINGMAN. Yes, sir; the water escaping through the Nita Crevasse reached the Gulf by the way of Lake Ponchartrain and the Rigolets.

This Morganza Crevasse was a mile in width, and the level of its bottom was such that when the river attained the height of some 30 to 35 feet above low water, the water overflowed through the crevasses. The first break occurred here, I think in 1874, and remained open until 1884, when it was closed up, but only remained closed for a few months, when it broke again and continued as a crevasse. In the winter of 1886 and 1887 the State of Louisiana and the United States began the construction of a levee to close the opening. While the work was in progress of construction, and before the river had risen high enough to reach the base of the levee, so that its effect would be felt on the regimen of the river, I measured a number of cross-sections in the vicinity and compared them with similar cross-sections taken by the Mississippi River Commission 3 years before, in 1883. I was therefore aware of the changes that had taken place from 1883 to 1886. This was a portion of the river which had been subject to the influence of an open crevasse for a number of years, and it showed that there had been a loss of effective area of cross-section of as much as 25 per cent. in the 3 years covered by the comparison, showing that the effect was a continuous and progressive deterioration of the channel. The year the levee was finished we had a flood of moderate height, but sufficient to develop the full influence of the levee. After the flood I repeated the soundings on all of the cross-sections and found that there had been a recovery of about 12½ per cent. For the next 2 years we had no water high enough to permit the levee to have any effect, and though I repeated the surveys, I found little or no change. The next year we had a very high flood, but unfortunately the levee broke. I do not know what has been the effect upon the channel since. I venture to predict, however, that an examination would show that the cross-section has again diminished. There was always water enough here for the purpose of navigation, but the crevasse was in a bend on the concave side. This caused the opposite point to project and made the bend rough and ugly. Pilots have told me that they dreaded it, and considered it one of the worst places on the lower river during low water. After the levee was built the conditions there greatly improved, and the low-water channel became entirely satisfactory. There was a case where the construction of a levee prevented injury to the channel and improved navigation. That was all that was done there, and was all that was necessary. I know many other similar cases could be, pointed out where the construction of a levee was all that was required to improve the navigation of the river at the particular point. I do not know that it is necessary to say anything further on that subject.

The first and most important question in regard to the construction of a system of levees on the Mississippi river from Cairo to the forts is this : Can a system be constructed which will be able to restrain any flood likely to occur? It is, in my opinion, perfectly practicable to do so, and at a moderate expense. It is just as practicable a problem as it would be to construct a railroad from Cairo to New Orleans, which nobody doubts can be done. I think that some engineers when asked whether a system can be constructed that will restrain any flood, have in their answers had several things in mind. They have had in their minds, particularly the care, or rather the lack of care, that these works when built once, ordinarily receive in time of low water. The only time that they ever do receive any repairs or any care, is in time of flood when they are greatly threatened, and then the repairs, though expensive, are hurriedly made, and are of little or no permanent value. If anybody should ask, "Is it possible to build a railroad from Cairo to New Orleans?" Of course the answer would be in the affirmative; but if it were asked, "Is it possible to build a railroad from Cairo to New Orleans, capable of sustaining a heavy traffic, without ever receiving any repairs?" The answer would probably be "No." Anything exposed to the action of rain and frost, and to the work of burrowing creatures, such as crawfish and beavers, as a levee is, must be carefully looked after. The weeds must be cut, the gulleys filled, and these burrowing creatures must be killed, and their work undone. If that is done, and a moderate amount of watchfulness and care is taken, such as is exercised by railroad companies in looking after their track, it would be more than sufficient to maintain a good system of levees when once built, and to enable it to successfully resist any flood in the river that is ever likely to occur.

The CHAIRMAN. Is there any engineering difficulty, in your judgment, in constructing levees on the bank of a stream, in protecting the bank at those points where there is erosion going on.

Captain KINGMAN. No; there would be no engineering difficulty, but there would be some expense. The great cost of the levee system to the States and to the United States has been due to the loss of levees in consequence of the caving of the river bank. Since 1882 the State of Louisiana has expended about $6,000,000 in the construction of levees, and the United States has expended about $2,500,000 for levees in the State of Louisiana, as roughly estimated. Of the $6,000,000 expended by the State, three-fourths was required for the construction of levees to replace others that had caved into the river, and the new levees were not any better than those they had replaced. All the money expended by the United States was for a similar purpose. And therefore we have, out of an expenditure of more than $8,000,000, only about $1,500,000 available for the improvement of the system. If *all* of that money could have been used in improving the system, the State would have had as good a system of levees as it would ever require. It would have been ample to afford complete protection from overflows. I am satisfied of this by my own experience.

* * * * * * * * * * * *

The CHAIRMAN. Of course you must protect the banks from caving, in order to protect the levees. I observed in going down the river that the current, or channel, changed constantly or went from one side to the other, and it would strike or impinge against one bank and the water would then be thrown across to the other.

Now, you protect the bank where the stream impinges and you protect it below on the opposite side. What I want to know, is there any danger of the channel changing entirely at these points so that the protection would be of no service and the river would strike at other points, and you would finally have to revet the entire bank on both sides?

Captain KINGMAN. I do not think there would be any danger of that on a thoroughly improved river; that is to say, on a river where the floods were controlled by a proper levee system, and where all of the caving bends had been revetted and given a proper form. But taking the river as it now is, if only two or three adjacent bends were protected, I should be afraid that the work might not be permanent, but that after two or three floods the points of the attack might be shifted below the protected portions. Still the influence of a single improved reach like that at Plum Point is felt in diminished caving for a long distance below.

LEVEES OF THE MISSISSIPPI RIVER.

REPORT OF ENGINEERS.

VICKSBURG, MISS., April 30, 1890.

To the Committee on Resolutions of the Mississippi
Improvement and Levee Convention:

Your committee, to whom was assigned the duty of preparing a statement on the subject of levees, beg leave to submit the following:

The testimony of all engineers familiar with the subject is that there is no engineering difficulty in the way of restraining the floods of the Mississippi river through the agency of levees, and that this is the only agency through which that object can be accomplished. The levees, as they existed at the beginning of the recent flood, were admittedly too weak generally, in height and width, to stand an extraordinary high water, as was recognized and affirmed by all levee engineers.

The fundamental defect in the present system of levee building is that they have not been designed and constructed on engineering principles, in the most thorough manner, with the sole view to certain efficiency, as is the case in all other classes of engineering work; but it has always been a mere question of doing the best that could be done with an insufficient amount of money.

The great desideratum has been to pile up as much dirt as possible in the cheapest possible way, so as to cover the greatest extent of territory with the highest bank of earth obtainable with the means at hand. This consideration has precluded such treatment of the foundations as the character and service of the structures demanded, to which deficiency is attributed much of their failure to successfully resist the extraordinary pressure of this flood at various points. The disasters from the recent flood

APPENDIX. 161

have been exaggerated and magnified beyond their true proportions by the sensational treatment which the subject has received, and which has tended to shake confidence in the efficiency of the levee system.

In confirmation of this attention is invited to the following facts: In 1882 the total number of crevasses in the levees was 284, aggregating 56.09 miles in width; in 1883 the number of crevasses was 224, with an aggregate width of 34.1 miles; in 1884 the crevasses numbered 204, aggregating 10.64 miles in width.

The result of crevasses enumerated during these three years was a general overflow of the Mississippi Delta. In the present flood, the dangers of which are nearly passed, the crevasses which have occurred number 23, aggregating about 4½ miles in width, in a total length of 1,100 miles of levees, or less than one-half of one per cent. of the total line of levees, notwithstanding that the present flood has exceeded those of the three years cited in the height attained at Memphis and all points below, and has not been exceeded in duration. This excess of height was, at Memphis 0.5 foot, at Helena 0.6 foot, at Sunflower Landing 1.2 feet, at Arkansas City 2.3 feet, at Greenville 1.7 feet, at Providence 3.1 feet, at Vicksburg 0.1 foot, at Natches 0.8 foot, and at New Orleans 0.5 foot. The general result has been a large measure of protection afforded by the levees this year, notwithstanding the extraordinary character of the flood, which has never been enjoyed during previous high waters of considerable magnitude.

For example, in the Yazoo Basin between 80 and 85 per cent. of its area is protected from overflow, there being only one crevasse of 280 feet in width, affecting a very small area, in 180 miles of levee extending from the upper extremity southward. There were other crevasses on this front below this locality. On the Tensas Front are two reaches of continuous levee, being respectively 81 and 135 miles in length. The right bank below Red river has 180 miles of continuous unbroken levee, and the left bank has 200 miles with only one break. Of the territory dependent upon the last-named levees, 75 per cent. has been protected. The percentages of areas protected as above noted embrace all classes of lands subject to overflow; as the lands sought for cultivation are the more elevated portions, the percentage of their area protected is much greater.

From our knowledge of this subject we now feel justified in declaring that very great progress has been made during the past 5 years in the construction of a complete levee system by the joint efforts of the general Government and the riparian States,; and also that the experience of the present flood has strongly added to our conviction that such a system presents the only solution of the protection of the alluvial valley from inundation, in connection with the general improvement of the river. We unhesitatingly express our condemnation of all theories for the regulation of the Mississippi river and controlling its floods by the agency of "outlets;" it is our conviction that such a system would prove destructive to all the interests which are sought to be conserved and improved in connection with the treatment of the Mississippi river. We also state with thorough conviction and emphasis, that the belief entertained by some that the effect of long confinement of the Mississippi river by levees will be to produce a permanent elevation of the river bed, is a fallacious one, which is refuted by experience and contrary to all observation. We are familiar with all surveys that have been made of the Mississippi and with its present navigation, and declare that there is no evidence from either of these sources, or elsewhere, of progressive elevation of the bed of the Mississippi river from levees or other cause, except where caused by, and immediately below, outlets.

We submit the following information relating to expenditures upon the levees from the following sources:

By the United States Government, through the Mississippi river Commission, since 1882................ $ 3,018,601.50
The Mississippi Levee Boards since 1882............. 3,098,745.74
State and levee districts of Louisiana, since 1866.... 15,255,327.13
Of which since 1882 about........................... 5,000,000.00
Arkansas.. 340,417.00

The above do not include expenditures which have been made by counties, corporations, and individuals in the several States. We estimate that a further expenditure of $10,000,000 by the general Government in co-operation with the riparian States, if promptly applied, will suffice to complete a system of levees that will prove entirely effective to restrain all future floods of the Mississippi river.

B. M. HARROD, C. E.
J. H. WILLARD,
Capt. Engineers, U. S. A.
W. YOUNG,
Capt. Engineers, U. S. A.
S. W. FERGUSON, C. E.
HENRY B. RICHARDSON, C. E.
WM. STARLING, C. E.
T. G. DABNEY, C. E.
H. S. DOUGLAS, C. E.
ARTHUR HIDER, C. E.
H. BOLIVAR THOMPSON, C. E.
H. ST. L. COPPEE, C. E.
JOHN SMYTH, C. E.
HENRY GOODRICH, C. E.
JOHN EWENS, C. E.
GEORGE M. HELM, C. E.
HORACE MARSHALL, C. E.

EXTRACTS FROM RESOLUTIONS OF COMMERCIAL CONGRESSES, COMMERCIAL ORGANIZATIONS AND LEGISLATURES OF STATES.

[NOTE.—From all portions of the United States have come strong resolutions requesting action by Congress, favorable to the improvement and leveeing of the Mississippi river. A few of the most important are given.—ED.]

RESOLUTION OF THE MISSOURI LEGISLATURE—1899.

Resolved, That it affords a great gratification to the people of the great West and the Mississippi valley to see the growing disposition throughout the Union to recognize the simple justice of aid being rendered by the Government in the construction and maintenance of levees, thus protecting and relieving the people of the lower valley from the disaster of the overflows.

It is peculiarly proper at this time to urge the passage of the Burrows bill, or a similar bill, by Congress, which bill appropriates $10,000,000, expending $3,000,000 annually for the building and maintenance of levees. In this connection we refer with pleasure to the work of the Mississippi River Commission, which has more than doubled the low-water depths on that portion of the Mississippi river where the Commission has done its work, and we indulge in the hope that this great and meritorious work will not be neglected by Congress, but pressed to a successful completion.

FROM THE NEW YORK CHAMBER OF COMMERCE.

Resolved, That this Chamber regards the continued overflow of our great inland sea, the Mississippi river, carrying with them loss of life and property, and devastation of most fertile regions, as a national disaster.

Resolved, That we respectfully request the President of the United States to bring this important matter to the attention of Congress; and we most earnestly urge upon Congress the wisdom and importance of adopting promptly such measures as experience, the results of the Mississippi River Commission and the judgment of the United States Corps of Engineers shall determine to be needed to create a permanent protection against the overflows of the river, and that the required appropriation of money to at once begin and finally complete those measures be made by Congress at this session.

Resolved, That a copy of these resolutions be sent to the Chamber of Commerce of our sister cities throughout the United States, and that they are hereby respectfully requested to take such action as the importance of this great subject demands.

Resolved, That a copy of these resolutions and the petition to this Chamber in reference to this subject be sent to the President and to each member of the Senate and House of Representatives of the United States and to the Press of the country, and that the chairman appoint a committee of nine, (9) of which he shall be chairman ex-officio, to go to Washington and personally lay this matter before the President and Congress.

Respectfully submitted,

(*Signed*,) A. FOSTER HIGGINS,
EDWARD HINCKEN,
JAMES S. T. STRANAHAN,
JOHN H. STARIN,
VERNON H. BROWN,
} Committee on the Harbor and Shipping.

NEW YORK, *June* 3, 1890.

The foregoing Report and Resolutions were unanimously adopted by the Chamber of Commerce at its monthly meeting, held June 5, 1890, and the following named gentlemen were appointed a Committee to lay the matter before the President and Congress:

CHARLES S. SMITH,
CHAUNCEY M. DEPEW,
CORNELIUS N. BLISS,
EDWARD H. AMMIDOWN,
JOHN SLOANE,

JOHN H. INMAN,
A. FOSTER HIGGINS,
RICHARD T. WILSON,
J. EDWARD SIMMONS,
CHARLES WATROUS.

Attest: GEORGE WILSON, Secretary.

FROM RESOLUTIONS ADOPTED BY THE UPPER MISSISSIPPI RIVER CONVENTION HELD AT DUBUQUE, IOWA.

Resolved, 1. That the important interests which this Convention has assembled to consider are now and have been for years entitled to the earnest consideration and watchful care of Congress and of the Chief Executive, to whom is entrusted, by the Constitution and the laws passed pursuant thereto, the advancement of the general welfare.

Upon all the products of the Northwest there is levied every year a direct and ruinous tax by way of increased freights, large insurance, demurrage, wrecks and repairs, caused by rocks, sand bars, snags and other obstacles to the safe and regular navigation of the Mississippi river.

No exercise of the power of Congress or of the Executive Prerogative can be more wise or just than the relief extended to the river commerce of the country and the varied interests which support it, by removing permanently and speedily all obstacles to navigation.

2. That the failure to make regular and adequate appropriations for the improvement of the Mississippi river meets with the earnest disapproval of this Convention, and we hereby invoke Congress to take prompt action during its present session upon this measure, to the end that ample time may be given for a full scrutiny of its provisions when executive action is demanded.

KANSAS CITY COMMERCIAL EXCHANGE.

The following resolutions were passed by the Commercial Exchange, July 19th, 1890:

Resolved, That the Mississippi river is the property of the Nation, the government having exclusive admirality jurisdiction over it; that it is the duty of the government to control the flood waters which have poured down from half the continent upon the States of Arkansas, Louisiana and Mississippi.

Resolved, That all the people in the United States are interested in the proper improvement and protection of the Mississippi river, because it is to-day the great continuing agency that controls

APPENDIX. 167

the freight rates on all the trunk line railroads East, West, North and South.

Resolved, That we, the Commercial Exchange, in behalf of Kansas City, ask Congress to make an appropriation of ten million dollars at the present Congress, being the amount asked by the River Commission/Engineers, to be available from year to year until the waters of this river are controlled at high floods, which will insure the best conditions of navigation at low water.

Resolved, That a copy of these resolutions be telegraphed to the President of the United States and our Senators in Congress and the member from this district.

MERCHANTS EXCHANGE OF ST. LOUIS.

ST. LOUIS, April 18, 1890.

Whereas, The attention of this body has been directed to the present disastrous results of overflow throughout many sections of the lower Mississippi valley, sections renowned for the productive power of their soil, from which valuable crops are gathered and vast sums thereby annually added to the nation's wealth by reason of the export character of these productions; and,

Whereas, Such inundations are not confined to lands bordering on the river, but spread over many miles of adjacent territory, thus proving so far reaching in their character and possibilities for destruction as to bring them properly within the scope of a national calamity, such as must earnestly appeal and emphatically for a nationalized remedy; therefore,

Resolved, That the unprecedented flood of the present year, now sweeping over many of the richest portions of the Mississippi valley, carrying ruin and devastation to large areas within the States of Mississippi, Arkansas and Louisiana, and bringing suffering and injury to a large portion of our people, must surely, in our judgment, impose upon the General Government an imperative duty to assist with its strong arm.

1. To repair the crippled condition of the works heretofore erected and maintained by a most burdensome system of local taxation.

2. To extend whatever aid may be found consistent with legislation under the Constitution, to prevent a recurrence of similar disaster.

Resolved, That while we commend the successful efforts of these people, through a series of years, to confine these annual floods to their proper channel, yet we realize that the partial failure to prevent inundation during the present phenomenal flood, only emphasizes the necessity of increased means and a more extended system of works; and in view of the vast extent of dependent, territory and population, we feel that to necessity is imparted a national character.

Resolved, That in recognition of the courageous spirit and just demand of the resolutions adopted by the people of the overflowed district at Greenville, Miss.,—the very center of disaster—and at Vicksburg and Memphis, we confidently appeal to our Senators and Representatives in Congress to use their best efforts for the eminently just and obligatory action of the Government in according the necessary aid to the end that not only the frequent excessive floods, but such unprecedented phenomenal floods as the present one, shall flow unvexed and harmless to the Gulf.

THE INTER-STATE MISSISSIPPI RIVER IMPROVEMENT AND LEVEE CONVENTION, HELD AT VICKSBURG, MISS., MAY 1ST, 1890.

Whereas, The duty and obligation is imposed by the Constitution upon the Federal Government of controlling and regulating commerce among the States, and jurisdiction is also given it over the navigable waters of the country; and on the lower Mississippi, under its constitutional direction the construction and maintenance of levees has been adopted as a means of flood confinement and navigation improvement.

This flood confinement and navigation improvement therefore subserves a dual purpose, to-wit: Improvement of navigation and the reclamation of the Mississippi Delta.

In view of this fact, their cost and control has been in the past divided between the General Government and the Levee Authorities of the various Levee Districts in the lower Mississippi valley. This principle of co-operation in the work of levee building, recognizing a community of interests between the United States Government and the people of the Delta, which has been inaugurated by the Mississippi River Commission, and given practical effect in the distribution of funds from this work, received the endorsement of President Arthur in his special message to Congress during 1883, and has recently received the emphatic approval of his Excellency President Harrison.

In the light of nine years' experience, the Mississippi River Commission and the United States Engineers jointly in charge of the work, have affirmed their faith in the plan by the tests of results and success. Therefore, we, the people of the Mississippi valley, in convention assembled, interested in the ultimate success of this work in both of its phases, now reaffirm our faith in this plan,' and express our willingness to continue in the future to pay our fair share of the expense of building and maintaining said levees, and through our Levee Organizations, to co-operate with the River Commission.

And by way of further endorsement of the Mississippi River Commission and their plan, we quote, with emphatic approval, from the resolutions of the Mississippi and Ohio River Pilot's Society, passed at St. Louis, April 25th, 1890, and submitted to this convention, as follows:

"*Whereas*, The present is the only complete system of levees we have ever had between Cairo and New Orleans, thus affording for the first time (up to the time said levees gave way under the flood) an opportunity of proving the engineers were correct; and,

"*Whereas*, We observed a greatly increased current, caused by said levees confining the surplus water to the natural channel, thereby clearly showing that this is the quickest way to get rid of the surplus water, while at the same time the friction is greater in the bottom than on the bank, in flood tide, as banks cave very little when they are full, the water acting as a support to save banks."

The national character and national importance of this problem, as well as the nation's duty in regard to it, is shown in the fact that the Mississippi valley and river is the receptacle and channel to the sea for the entire drainage from twenty-five States and Territories between the Alleghaney and the Rocky mountains. This drainage is in each succeeding year precipitated into this channel more rapidly by reason of the changed and changing settlement and cultivation of many States about the headwaters.

Furthermore, we recite that the Mississippi river is a prime factor in controlling for the best interests of the whole people of the Union the transportation rates of the whole country, and that there is a greater obstruction to commerce by the floods than by low water, by reason of the impossibility of access to the river in times of overflow.

Resolved, That it is the deliberate judgment of this convention that the "outlet theory" of improvement of the Mississippi river is impracticable, and would be ultimately destructive of both navigation and the alluvial territory bordering the Mississippi river.

Resolved, That we receive with great satisfaction the unqualified endorsement of the plan of the Mississippi River Commission for the improvement of the Mississippi river by the use of levees by the Merchants' Exchange of St. Louis, the New Orleans Board of Trade, the Commercial Club of Louisville, and the Mississippi River and Ohio Pilot's Society, as shown by their resolutions submitted to this convention; and that they concur in the opinion of this convention that if the United States Government would make a liberal appropriation for the construction of larger and stronger levees on the banks of said river, that said plan would then approximate perfection, and that the channel of said river would be improved for the purposes of commerce, the alluvial lands on the banks of said river be protected from overflow, and the Government spared the annual outlay made by it for the repair of crevasses and the relief of individual suffering occasioned by inundation.

Resolved, That the free, perennial navigation of our great rivers, wherever possible to be effected by legislation, should be demanded of the Government and receive its attention as promptly and as unstintedly as harbor improvements on the Atlantic, Pacific, Gulf or Lake coasts.

That the recent floods in the lower Mississippi, which have proven to be beyond control of the most determined State, municipal, district and county efforts combined, should emphasize once more the great fact, always true, and heretofore always overlooked, that the Mississippi river is the nation's river, or, as called by one of the greatest strict constructionists of the Constitution, the nation's great "Inland Sea," and as such it "comes as much within the purview of the Constitution as do the harbors of the Atlantic, Pacific, Gulf or Lake coasts."

NATIONAL FARMERS' CONGRESS.

MACEDONIA, IOWA, Oct. 17, 1890.

Whereas, Water route competition is a most important factor in the regulation and cheapening of transportation charges upon our products for distant markets, and the least liable to the control of combines and pools ; therefore be it

Resolved, That we demand of Congress most liberal appropriations for the improvement, by all practicable means, of our interior waterways, which shall make them, instead of sources of disaster and destruction to large sections of our country, useful as great national highways for the commerce and trade of our products."

I hereby certify that the above is a true copy of the resolution as passed by the Ninth Annual Session of the National Farmers' Congress at Council Bluffs, Iowa, August 26-29, 1890.

B. F. CLAYTON, Secretary.

THE DAVENPORT BUSINESS MEN'S ASSOCIATION.

"*Resolved*, By the Davenport Business Men's Association, that we favor the improvement of the lower Mississippi as set forth in the bill now pending before Congress, appropriating $9,000,000 to "levee the Mississippi from Cairo to the Gulf."

HENRY T. DENISON, Secretary.

THE CHAMBER OF COMMERCE AND INDUSTRY, OF LOUISIANA.

Resolved, That this boards notes with gratification the growing disposition through the Union to recognize the simple justice of aid being rendered by the general government in the construction and maintenance of the Mississippi river, our great natural waterway, and partially relieving the inhabitants of the lower valley of the gigantic hardship and burden of protecting their lives and property from the annual incursion of floods passed down on them from no less than 23 States. While gratefully acknowledging the need of succor already extended by Congress, and the Mississippi River Commission in this direction, we earnestly ask that a fuller measure of justice be done by more adequate provision for the establishment of a levee system that will prevent a recurrence of such dire calamities as the overflows of 1890, 1884, 1882, 1874, and many previous years. We particularly solicit from Congress favorable action upon the bill proposing to appropriate $9,000,000 for building the levees along the Mississippi river, and feel confident the sentiment of the country will justify and applaud the expenditure of public money in such a meritorious and truly national work.

THE LOUISVILLE BOARD OF TRADE.

The necessity for the early improvement of the Mississippi river and its principal tributaries, when considered in connection with the completion and use of the Nicarauga Canal.

Whereas, The Mississippi river and its tributaries constitute the greatest and most valuable highway for commerce in the world, reaching the trade of nearly every State of the Union; and

Whereas, the construction of a ship canal across the American isthmus at Nicaragua will greatly add to the value of this highway by causing it to practically empty into both oceans; therefore, be it

Resolved, That it is the duty of the United States Government without delay to provide for the improvement, and continued maintenance of such improvement, of the Mississippi river and its principal branches, to the end that as far as practicable their navigation may be free and unannoyed to the sea.

THE WESTERN COMMERCIAL CONGRESS.

Resolved, That the waterways of a country are nature's arteries of commercial circulation, and the people's surest safeguard against railway combinations and railway pooling, and the best of all possible guarantees of cheap transportation; and

Resolved, That it is the duty of the National Government to pursue a liberal policy for the improvement of the waterways of the country.

APPENDIX. 173

Resolved, That the Mississippi river and its affluents should receive the special care of the government and ample appropriations from time to time should be made to carry out the improvements already begun under the Mississippi and Missouri River Commissioners, the completion and perfection of the levee system from St. Paul to the sea, and the maintenance of navigable channels in all of the tributaries of said rivers, in so far as the same may be practicable.

* * * * * * * * * * * * *

Resolved, That in the judgment of this Congress the Mississippi river can be and should be made navigable for ocean steamers of such class as now enter the port of New Orleans for a considerable distance above that port, and that without attempting to make a point or fix a limit to said ship navigation, we earnestly recommend to the National Congress the early passage of a measure similar to the one known as the Burrows bill, which provided an appropriation of $10,000,000 to be used in the construction of levees from St. Paul to the Gulf, thereby deepening the channel of the river and protecting millions of acres of the richest lands in the world.

STATE OF ILLINOIS, 37TH GENERAL ASSEMBLY,
HOUSE OF REPRESENTATIVES,

ILLINOIS, April 11, 1891.

Whereas, The unobstructed navigation of the Mississippi river is a matter of national interest, and in view of its influence in regulating freight rates is of special importance to producers in the Western and Northern States; and,

Whereas, The annually recurring overflows of that river, destroying both life and property and devastating most fertile regions, are disasters detrimental to the national prosperity; and,

Whereas, Recent experience has demonstrated that by the system of improvement of the stream adopted by the Mississippi River Commission, the river floods can be controlled and the navigation of the river be made safe and certain at all seasons of the year; therefore,

Resolved, That Congress is respectfully urged to make an appropriation of money sufficient in amount to complete the system of improvement of the Mississippi river adopted by the Mississippi River Commission and recommended by the United States corps of engineers ; and be it

Resolved, That the members of the National House of Representatives and United States Senators from this State be notified of the action of this body upon this resolution.

TRANS-MISSISSIPPI CONGRESS, DENVER, COL., MAY 19, 1891.

Whereas, The Mississippi river and its navigable tributaries constitute the most valuable natural highway for the commerce of the country to the sea, and reaches the trade of nearly every State and Territory west of the Mississippi river; and

Whereas, The permanent improvement of the Mississippi river and its navigable tributaries will insure stable and regular rates throughout the year by competition with the trunk lines to the seaboard ; therefore be it

Resolved, That it is the duty of the United States Government to provide adequate and continuous appropriations for the improvement of the Mississippi river and principal tributaries, so as to secure safe and free navigation on these rivers; and be it further

Resolved, That it affords great gratification to the people of the great West and the Mississippi valley to see the growing disposition throughout the Union to recognize the simple justice of aid being rendered by the government in the construction and maintenance of levees, thus protecting and relieving the people of the lower valley from the disaster of the overflows.

It is peculiarly proper at this time to urge the passage of the Burrows' bill, or a similar bill, by Congress, which bill appropriates $10,000,000, expending $3,000,000 annually, for the building and maintenance of levees. In this connection we refer with pleasure to the work of the Mississippi River Commission, which has more than doubled the low-water depths on that portion of the Mississippi river where the Commission has done its work, and we indulge in the hope that this great and meritorious work will not be neglected by Congress, but pressed to a successful completion.

RESOLUTION MISSISSIPPI DEMOCRATIC CONVENTION,

JULY 15, 1891.

Resolved, That we believe that every legitimate power of the Government should be exerted to provide the people with cheaper facilities for transportation, inasmuch as a large portion of the earnings is now taken from them to pay the cost of marketing their products; we therefore demand liberal appropriations by Congress for the improvement of our rivers and harbors, regarding their improvement as an absolutely essential step toward the accomplishment of the desired end.

www.ingramcontent.com/pod-product-compliance
Lightning Source LLC
Chambersburg PA
CBHW020301170426
43202CB00008B/453